MEMOIRS OF THE
AMERICAN FOLKLORE SOCIETY

VOLUME 45
1954

NORTH AMERICAN INDIAN
MUSICAL STYLES

By
BRUNO NETTL

PHILADELPHIA
AMERICAN FOLKLORE SOCIETY
1954

THE WILLIAM BYRD PRESS, INC.
RICHMOND, VIRGINIA

PREFACE: HISTORY OF THE STUDY OF NORTH AMERICAN INDIAN MUSIC

THE history of the study of North American Indian music is closely tied to the history of comparative musicology at large. It served as the subject matter for the beginning of the science and has been a central branch of it since then. Although individual melodies, some of them perhaps in transcriptions reliable enough to be useful, were published earlier,[1] the first important studies were made after 1880. The earliest serious study is by Baker.[2] Written in Leipzig as a doctoral dissertation, it attempts to survey the entire field of North America and includes a number of transcriptions, partly by the author and partly quoted, made without the use of recordings. This study is primarily of historical interest.

The first study of the music of one tribe, using the accepted methods of comparative musicology, was made by Stumpf.[3] It includes nine songs transcribed without recordings. Later students almost invariably made use of phonograph recordings, which has improved the technique of transcribing immeasurably and has made possible the minute study of a song through several successive renditions, each of which may differ from the rest.

Among the American pioneers in North American Indian music, Gilman,[4] Fletcher,[5] and Fewkes[6] must be mentioned. Their works were somewhat isolated from those of their German contemporaries and are not in the usual tradition of comparative musicology. Many collections of Indian songs, transcribed, were also published, without any analytical discussion, by Curtis-Burlin[7] and Curtis[8] among others. Densmore[9] has described the study of Indian music in the nineteenth century.

Among the early German comparative musicologists relatively little was done in the field of North American Indian music. Their work was concentrated primarily on Oriental and Old World primitive music. One monograph of considerable size on the music of the Thompson River Indians was contributed by Abra-

[1] For example, Jean Jacques Rousseau, *Dictionnaire de Musique* (Paris, 1768), appendix, contains a Canadian Indian song.

[2] Theodor Baker, *Über die Musik der nordamerikanischen Wilden* (Leipzig, 1882).

[3] Carl Stumpf, "Lieder der Bellakula Indianer," *Vierteljahrschrift für Musikwissenschaft,* **2** (1886), 405-426.

[4] Benjamin Ives Gilman, "Hopi Songs," *Journal of American Ethnology and Archaeology,* **5** (1908), 1-160.

[5] Alice C. Fletcher, *A Study of Omaha Music* (Cambridge, 1893).

[6] J. W. Fewkes, "On the Use of the Phonograph among the Zuni Indians," *American Naturalist,* **24** (1890), 687-691.

[7] Natalie Curtis-Burlin, *The Indians' Book* (New York and London, 1907).

[8] Edward S. Curtis, *The North American Indian* (Norwood, Mass., 1907-1930), 20 vol.

[9] Frances Densmore, "The Study of Indian Music in the Nineteenth Century," *American Anthropologist,* **29** (1927), 68-77. See also Willard Rhodes, "North American Indian Music," *Notes,* **10** (1952), 33-45.

ham and Hornbostel,[10] two of the scholars most instrumental in developing the field of comparative musicology.

Although comparatively little in the way of analytical study was accomplished in America during the nineteenth and early twentieth centuries, a large amount of recording, often by musically untrained investigators, was done. This has been very fortunate for the students of Indian music today since much of this material which has disappeared in the native repertories is available for study now. In many ethnological and folkloristic treatises, as well as independently, transcriptions of songs were published without analysis or discussion of the musical style; they are often less accurate than those made by professional comparative musicologists, but they are usually adequate for gaining knowledge of the styles. Among the transcriptions of the nineteenth century, those published by Mooney,[11] Cringan,[12] and Matthews[13] are among the most important.

Franz Boas was responsible for encouraging the study of Indian music by his students. Although not trained in musicology, he was in close contact with Hornbostel and himself published transcriptions, made by himself and J. C. Fillmore, of Central Eskimo[14] and Kwakiutl[15] music.

During the first half of the twentieth century, aboriginal North America has become the continent of primitive cultures whose music has been the most extensively studied and is best known. This is the result of the publication of numerous transcriptions as well as a number of comparative studies of limited areas. The three most important workers in the field of North America have been Frances Densmore, Helen H. Roberts, and George Herzog. Densmore has been the most prolific; her merit is primarily that of a collector. She is responsible for about half of the transcriptions published so far, and for the largest collections printed from single tribes.[16] She has concentrated largely on the Plains Indians and some tribes in their vicinity. Her transcriptions are generally good, although not as detailed as they should be for maximum usefulness.[17] Her rhythmic divisions are often questionable; they appear to have been made under too much influence of traditional European music theory which favors isometric construction, and the Indian melodies have been forced into this framework. In the preparation of the present study, although Densmore's transcriptions have been used extensively for analysis, it has often been necessary to ignore her bar-lines and to draw new ones. Thus,

[10] Otto Abraham and Erich M. von Hornbostel, "Phonographierte Indianermelodien aus Britisch Columbia," in *Boas Anniversary Volume* (New York, 1906), pp. 447-474.

[11] James Mooney, *The Ghost-Dance Religion and the Sioux Outbreak of 1890* (Washington, 1896).

[12] Alexander T. Cringan, "Music of the Pagan Iroquois," *Archaeological Report,* Appendix to the Report of the Minister of Education (Toronto, 1899), pp. 166-189.

[13] Washington Matthews, *Navaho Legends* (New York, 1897).

[14] Franz Boas, *The Central Eskimo* (Washington, 1888).

[15] Boas, *The Social Organization and the Secret Societies of the Kwakiutl Indians* (Washington, 1897).

[16] Frances Densmore, *Chippewa Music* (Washington, 1910) and *Chippewa Music II* (Washington, 1913), together constitute the largest collection published from one tribe, comprising 340 songs.

[17] A number of recordings made by Densmore have been made available to the public by the Library of Congress. It has been possible to check the transcriptions of these songs in her publications.

Densmore's analysis of Indian music leans perhaps too heavily on European music; it tries to measure Indian music by European standards. While this is admittedly unavoidable in certain instances, it is believed that, for example, the classification of pentatonic scales according to major and minor, the identification of major and minor thirds as equivalent (simply because both are called thirds), and the designation of important tones in the scales, such as tonics, by their position in a European major or minor scale rather than by their function in the songs themselves, are subject to criticism. Nevertheless, Densmore's monumental achievements in collecting and transcribing, as well as her descriptions of musical instruments, singers, and customs pertaining to music, must be recognized as a prime and unique contribution.

Helen H. Roberts, besides contributing a number of works on the styles of individual tribes and small areas such as the Copper Eskimo[18] and the Indians of Southern California,[19] is responsible for the only previous attempt to show the entire picture of North American Indian music. Her study of musical areas in aboriginal North America[20] does not make full use of the material available at the time it was written. Although the present writer has found that most of her statements coincide, on the whole, with his findings, they are presented in rather unsystematic fashion, with little detail and much impressionistic material. She does not give statements of frequency and does not always indicate the tribes within an area whose music she has examined. Her musical areas are, in some cases, not musical areas in the sense of the word used here; they are culture areas whose musical styles are relatively homogeneous. She approaches the problem with the culture area as the point of departure. Thus, although her statements are usually reliable, she has produced a study which, on the whole, does not describe musical areas but the musical styles of culture areas. There are exceptions to the latter statement: she combines the styles of the Pueblo and some Plains Indians which belong to different culture areas. Roberts also relies considerably on the descriptions of Indian music by early writers while placing less emphasis on the available transcriptions. Since it is known that many statements by early writers and travelers remain unsubstantiated, her picture is, at times, unrealistic. In spite of these criticisms, the writer hastens to state that he considers Roberts' study among the most important in the field, that he has made much use of it, and that without it the preparation of this study would have been much more difficult.

George Herzog is responsible for most of the comparative studies in North American Indian music to date. In a short, early article he gave the general picture of the continent with the vocal technique as the chief criterion of differentiation.[21] He has produced a comparison of Southwestern styles,[22] a comparative study of Northwest coast music,[23] and a discussion of some archaic song types throughout

[18] Helen H. Roberts and Diamond Jenness, *Songs of the Copper Eskimo* (Ottawa, 1925).

[19] Roberts, *Form in Primitive Music* (New York, 1933).

[20] Roberts, *Musical Areas in Aboriginal North America* (New Haven, 1936).

[21] George Herzog, "Musical Styles in North America," *Proceedings of the 23rd International Congress of Americanists,* (1928), 455-458.

[22] Herzog, "A Comparison of Pueblo and Pima Musical Styles," *JAF,* **49** (1938), 283-417.

[23] Herzog, "Salish Music," in Marian W. Smith, ed., *Indians of the Urban Northwest* (New York, 1949), pp. 93-110.

the continent.[24] Herzog's work includes accurate, detailed transcriptions and analysis in accordance with the traditions of comparative musicology. Material on song texts and the cultural background of music, often scanty in other publications, is also included by him.

Although the studies of comparative musicologists have been primarily concerned with synchronic descriptions of musical styles, the fact that North American Indian music is so well known makes it possible to begin the work of reconstructing the history of some of the styles and tribes, and to show the processes of musical change occurring in acculturational situations. This can be done by correlating musical and other cultural data and has been attempted occasionally, mainly with recent changes. Herzog[25] has traced the movement of a style from the Great Basin to the Plains in the nineteenth century. The writer[26] has placed in possible chronological order the four sub-styles of Shawnee music. Reconstruction of music history going back several centuries has been attempted by Estreicher.[27] Hornbostel[28] made some tentative statements about the musical style of the Indians before and after their arrival in the New World. This type of study in the field of musical prehistory is possible only because of the relatively large amount which is known about Indian music and has rarely, and with less success, been attempted for other continents.

The work of recording, as well as the published material, has not been distributed evenly over the continent. Some areas have been covered extensively while others have barely been approached. Best represented among the culture areas are the Plains, the Western part of the Woodlands, and the Prairies. The Northwest Coast, Southwest, and Eskimo have been well covered. Most of the remaining areas have been covered adequately for showing their positions in musical areas, but much material needs still to be recorded, transcribed, and analysed before definitive statements can be made. This is particularly true for the Northern Athabascans and the Eastern Algonquians, and to some extent it is true for the entire continent. It is perfectly conceivable that the present scheme of musical areas will have to be revised soon because of new finds.

This study is the bulk of the writer's doctoral dissertation, accepted by the Graduate School of Indiana University in 1953. The writer wishes to thank his teachers and colleagues at Indiana University for their help and encouragement. He is especially indebted to George Herzog for introduction to and instruction in the methods, techniques, and content of comparative musicology. He is further indebted to Jody C. Hall for permission to use his manuscript material on Modoc music as a source of information, to Peter F. Abraham for furnishing a description

[24] Herzog, "Special Song Types in North American Indian Music," *Zeitschrift für vergleichende Musikwissenschaft,* 3 (1935), 23-33.

[25] Herzog, "Plains Ghost Dance and Great Basin Music," *American Anthropologist,* 37 (1935), 403-419.

[26] Bruno Nettl, "The Shawnee Musical Style: Historical Perspective in Primitive Music," *Southwestern Journal of Anthropology,* 9 (1953), 277-285.

[27] Zygmunt Estreicher, "Die Musik der Eskimos," *Anthropos,* 45 (1950), 659-720.

[28] Hornbostel, "Musik und Musikinstrumente," in Theodor Koch-Gruenberg, *Vom Roroima zum Orinoko* (Stuttgart, 1923), III, 397-442.

of Central California Indian music, and to Harold E. Driver for permission to use his tribal map of North America as the basis for the map of musical areas. This study, without preface and musical examples, was published in the JOURNAL OF AMERICAN FOLKLORE, **67** (1954), in three installments.[29]

[29] Because of this, certain dislocations in footnote numbering are inevitable; however, it is hoped that this will not seriously inconvenience the reader.

TABLE OF CONTENTS

NORTH AMERICAN INDIAN
MUSICAL STYLES

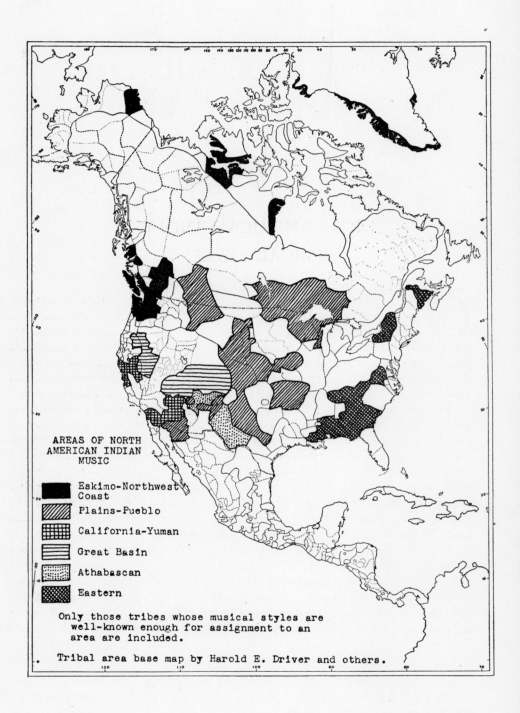

AREAS OF NORTH
AMERICAN INDIAN
MUSIC

- ◼ Eskimo-Northwest Coast
- ◩ Plains-Pueblo
- ▦ California-Yuman
- ▤ Great Basin
- ▦ Athabascan
- ▨ Eastern

Only those tribes whose musical styles are
well-known enough for assignment to an
area are included.

Tribal area base map by Harold E. Driver and others.

NORTH AMERICAN INDIAN MUSICAL STYLES

1. INTRODUCTION

OUR general problem is the distribution of musical style traits in American Indian music north of Mexico. Following are some of the main questions which we attempt to answer: are there some stylistic traits which are common to all of the music in the above-mentioned area; what are the geographic distributions of the most important style traits within this area; according to the distributions found, what musical areas may be delineated for North American Indian music; do the musical areas coincide with culture areas and linguistic areas?

The time may be ripe for a study which ties together the many tribal monographs on North American Indian music which have appeared in the last several decades, and which attempts to give, in some detail, the general picture. Although more musical material is available from this large area of primitive cultures than from any other of similar size, little has been done to survey the entire continent with the use of all the available material. Some early essays[1][2] represented the view that all Indian music had the same general style. Later it was thought that two major styles dominated the continent.[3] Today it is known that great complexity exists in the distribution of musical characteristics among the various tribes.

Two significant attempts to delimit musical areas in North America have been made. The first, by Herzog,[4] is a brief paper; the other is a lengthier one, by Roberts.[5] The latter is a monograph which is not very detailed, stresses the distribution of musical instruments and surveys the available material. Comparatively little emphasis is given to the distribution of stylistic features. Also, a great deal of material has become available since her work appeared.

---

[1][2] E. M. von Hornbostel, "Musik und Musikinstrumente," in Koch-Gruenberg, *Vom Roroima zum Orinoko* (Stuttgart, 1923), III, 397–442.

[3] George Herzog, "The Yuman Musical Style," *JAF,* 2 (1928), 183–231.

[4] Herzog, "Musical Styles in North America," *Proceedings of the 23rd International Congress of Americanists,* (1928), 455–458.

[5] Helen H. Roberts, *Musical Areas in Aboriginal North America* (Yale University Publications in Anthropology, 12, New Haven, 1936).

The present study surveys the musical styles of about 80 tribes whose music, it may be assumed, is a representative sample of most of the North American material, although hundreds of tribes remain untouched and unknown. The analyzed material has all been recorded within the last 70 years, but students of Indian music have usually assumed that its musical styles existed before 1500, although their distribution may have been somewhat different from their present ones. There seems to have been a minimum of hybridization of musical styles between European and American Indian cultures north of Mexico. However, the picture presented here refers specifically to music of the last century with recognition of the probability that it is much older. Musical styles which are known to have arisen and spread in recent decades are included as special examples of historical processes. Mexican Indian music is not included because it has largely disappeared or been assimilated into Spanish-American folk and popular music, and little is known of it. However, it is possible that from the distributions of musical traits north of Mexico some tentative conclusions can be drawn about the music of the ancient Mexican high cultures.

The raw material for this study consists, primarily, of transcriptions of melodies into musical notations. Three types of sources were used: about 60 published monographs and books, some of which also contained descriptions of styles; unpublished transcriptions, supplied by colleagues or made by the writer; and field recordings (mostly from the Archives of Folk and Primitive Music, Indiana University), used to corroborate the written material. The most important sources for each section of the country were gathered. Where there is much available material, only the largest collections were used, and where material is lacking, even some articles containing the transcription of only one song. The writer does not pretend to have exhausted the material; still, it is estimated that over 90 per cent of the published transcriptions of North American Indian music, in addition to many unpublished ones, were analyzed and form part of the picture presented.

The emphasis is on the technical aspects of musical style. The musical areas which are to be identified are areas of style and are not based on the distributions of musical instruments or features of the cultural background of music. The following sections give the stylistic features of the entire continent and of each musical area in some detail. A musical area may be defined as a geographic area whose inhabitants share in a generally homogeneous musical style. Such an area is unified by one or several important traits which are not found with the same degree of intensity in neighboring areas. To be sure, the styles of any two tribes differ in many respects, and it has been difficult to draw exact lines which delimit the areas. Musical areas could be identified at various degrees of homogeneity; each tribe, or even each sub-style within a tribal style, could be considered equivalent to a musical area by virtue of its contrast with the surrounding material. Again, the whole continent could be considered one musical area which contrasts with other large areas of primitive culture. Still it has been relatively easy to define the musical areas: most of them, as do Wissler's culture areas, have a center of development which is most typical and sometimes most complex. The number of musical areas approximates those of the culture areas of Wissler and Kroeber, although their specific boundaries do not coincide. The characteristics of culture areas are shared by the musical areas, but it has sometimes been necessary to leave unidentified the musical equivalents of the culture centers, as was done, according to Kroeber, by Wissler. In some larger musical areas it is useful to discuss smaller units within them—sub-areas—separately. Several sub-areas may fit together into one musical area, but they are distinguished by important features. While stylistic complexity has not been one of the criteria for differentiating musical areas, it has been used to distinguish the sub-areas of some of those areas.

Some tribes have been found to participate in almost equal degrees in the styles of two musical areas. Such tribes, e.g. the Northern Utes, Pima, Papago, and Shawnee, are usually located at the meeting-points of musical areas. Their styles are discussed in the sections devoted to those styles which seem dominant in their musical cultures, but they are designated as marginal to these areas.

A musical style is defined by statements of frequency—statistical statements—rather than by statements which indicate only the absolute presence or absence of a given trait. Indeed, while it is possible to state the presence of a trait in the material examined, it is unsafe to rely upon statements which indicate the complete absence of a trait in a given repertory, because the trait may appear in some as yet unrecorded material within the style. However, it is believed that the samples of music studied are representative enough to enable one to draw reliable conclusions about the relative frequency of the traits.

The methods of analyzing the Indian melodies used to identify the musical areas are those described by Hornbostel[6] and followed by Herzog.[7] The results are presented in the following order: melody, rhythm, form, and other features. The descriptions of the styles are primarily in terms of those traits by which they are differentiated. These are emphasized, while the others are discussed more briefly. Following is an explanation of the musicological techniques and terminology.

Under the category of melody falls discussion of range (the distance between the lowest and highest tones in a song), scale, and melodic movement. Scale is defined as all of the tones occurring in a given song, not including octave duplications. They are described by the number of tones in them (pentatonic, tetratonic, etc.), the most common intervals in them, and the position of the tonic and other important tones. These are placed according to their positions within the total range. Satisfaction of the greatest number of the following criteria determines the identity of the tonic: tone occurring most often during a song; tone occurring with sufficient length or duration to distinguish it from the others; tone occurring as the final tone of several units within a song; and final tone of the song. The last criterion is the most important, but the tonic usually satisfies two or three of the criteria.

The intervals of North American Indian music, generally speaking, approximate those of Western European music; thus the names of the latter are used. Exact measurements in terms of cents or vibration rates are usually not available; consequently the interval names indicate intervals relatively close to the Western equivalents of those names, but the intervals usually do not match exactly. It

[6] E. M. von Hornbostel, "Melodie und Skala," *Jahrbuch der Musikbibliothek Peters,* **19** (1913), 11–23.
[7] Herzog, 1928, p. 190.

appears that more leeway is allowed most Indian singers in the matter of intonation than is allowed European folk or art singers. Wherever such intervals as quarter-tones, used consistently, are indicated, they are described. The only additional term used is "neutral third" which indicates an interval intermediate between a major and minor third.

The movement of the melody in general is an important factor in determining musical areas. It is described in terms of the general contour as well as by indicating common melodic intervals.

The analysis of rhythm is based on the description of the durational values used, the meter, and the instrumental accompaniment. It has been useful to differentiate styles by the number of durational values (note values) used in individual songs. In some styles five or six values are found distributed about equally in number throughout a song. In others it has been found that, while the same total number exists, two or three values tend to dominate the song and the others appear only occasionally. In other styles, again, two note values are used almost exclusively. These distinctions are useful; they help to explain the apparent relative complexity and simplicity of different rhythmic styles. It has not been possible to make statements about the relative fixity or flexibility of rhythmic values since most of the analysis is based on transcriptions representing only one rendition of a given song. The same applies to relative flexibility in other aspects of musical style.

Meter, as determined by the regular placement of stresses, repetitions of series of note values, and repetition of melodic patterns, is classified as either isometric or heterometric. While purely isometric songs are exceedingly rare in North America, some styles have long stretches of isometric construction and others do not. The kinds of successions of note values, i.e. whether there are series of tones with the same note value or whether there is constant contrast, are also useful to differentiate some styles.

Isorhythmic construction is also discussed. While very few songs are strictly isorhythmic, many are partly so (they have long isorhythmic sections) and modified (isorhythmic with the exception of a few note values). The type of rhythmic accompaniment which is found in a musical area is described and its relationship to the rhythm of the melody is indicated.

In the discussion of form, the over-all structure is first described. It is classified as either strophic, if the entire song is repeated a number of times in performance, or throughcomposed. The approximate number of identifiable sections or phrases in each song is given as well as the approximate lengths of the sections and the entire songs. The relationship among the sections is indicated by the classification in one of the following three types: progressive (no material repeated), reverting (restatement of earlier material), and iterative (repetition of material immediately preceding). While each song is bound to have some progressive parts and all three types may be present in one song, a song can usually be characterized by one of these three types, as can an entire style.[8] Letters are used to symbolize the structural sub-divisions of the songs. Modification is indicated by ciphers: A^1 and A^2, for instance, are slightly different. For sections more distantly related, small letter

---

[8] For a fuller explanation of these terms, see Herzog, "A Comparison of Pueblo and Pima Musical Styles," *JAF*, 49 (1938), 305.

coefficients are used: for example, B^a is not merely a modified repetition of A; it is in some fashion related to A, in melodic contour perhaps, but it is relatively independent. A figure in parentheses following a letter indicates transposition: A(5) is A transposed down a perfect fifth. Upward transposition, because it is rare, is not included in this system.

Antiphonal technique, responsorial technique, and polyphony, wherever they are found, are discussed after form. The vocal technique, such as the use of vocal tension and pulsation as well as dynamics, accentuation, etc., are also treated. Mention of musical instruments is made according to the classification of Sachs and Hornbostel,[9] using the types idiophones (percussion instruments whose bodies vibrate), membranophones (drums with heads of skin), aerophones (wind-instruments), and chordophones (string instruments). In the identification of the tribes which belong to one musical area, only those whose styles are known are included. Although certain tribes which are located between member-tribes of one musical area could logically be considered a part of the same area, they are not included if their styles are not known.

There are a few traits which are common to all, or the vast majority, of North American Indian tribal styles. These traits are generalized; the more specific and specialized traits, such as cascading melodic movement and great vocal tension, which were once thought to be characteristic of all American Indian music, were found to have relatively limited distributions in the western hemisphere and to be present also in the Old World. In spite of this generalized character, however, the traits listed here serve to differentiate North American Indian music as a whole from other styles and to lend some degree of homogeneity to the music of this continent, however diverse it may be in other respects.

The basic unit in Indian music is the song, which usually lasts (including a number of repetitions where this is customary) between 20 seconds and three minutes. The vast majority of the songs are monophonic: they include only a melody and have only one pitch sounding at a given moment. Purely instrumental music is rare. There is no solo drumming, and the only melodic instrumental music is that played on flutes and flageolets. These are used by many tribes as love charms and in ceremonies. Most of the melodies played on them may also be sung. Those tribes having flute melodies at all possess only a few; a typical tribal repertory may consist of several hundred vocal songs and a dozen flute melodies. Whereas simultaneous playing on the flute and singing is not found, and ensemble music with more than one flute does not exist, the combination of percussive accompaniment with vocal music is almost universal in North America.

The range of the melodies is usually between a perfect fifth and a perfect twelfth. The majority (ca. 60 per cent) of the scales are pentatonic. The most common intervals in the scales as well as the melodies are major seconds and minor thirds; generally speaking, most of the intervals approximate those of the Western tempered scale. The final tones in the songs are usually the tonics, which are mostly the lowest tones of the individual songs.

[9] These terms were introduced by E. M. von Hornbostel and Curt Sachs, "Systematik der Musikinstrumente," *Zeitschrift für Ethnologie,* 46 (1914), 553–590.

The rhythm of North American Indian music is organized heterometrically; isometric construction is very rare. Isorhythmic construction, however, is found in some areas. The general rhythmic picture is one of relative complexity; it is complex even in the simpler North American styles. The forms of North American Indian music are usually strophic; noted exceptions to this occur on the West Coast. A strophe consists of between two and twelve separate sections which are usually also phrases (having some kind of cadential marker). These have a duration of between three and ten seconds and are of unequal lengths within an individual song. They tend to become longer towards the end of a strophe.

Among the types of instruments found in North America, the most common are idiophones. Membranophones and aerophones are also found in most tribes, but chordophones have a very limited distribution. The function of music is primarily religious. Men predominate in the musical activities of most areas; they lead the singing and compose the songs, and they are the makers and players of instruments. Group singing and solo singing are both common throughout the continent.

A characteristic which typifies North American Indian music is the predominance of meaningless syllable song texts. The majority of the Indian songs contain either entirely or partly meaningless syllables. Because of the paucity of text materials it is probably not possible to differentiate textual areas (except in subject matter, which is musicologically not relevant), and thus discussion of texts and text-music relationships are not included here.

2. THE ESKIMO-NORTHWEST COAST AREA

This area includes the Eskimo, the Northwest Coast, and the Salish tribes. It is rather well documented: only the Plains-Pueblo area exceeds it in the number of song transcriptions published. Roberts[10] recognizes the relationship between Eskimo style and that of the remainder of the area, but, following cultural lines, she discusses the Eskimo separately in her study of musical areas. The Eskimo-Northwest Coast area is characterized by the use of complex rhythmic organization and the use of recitative-like singing. The latter consists of the rhythmic recitation of a text with a melody whose general contour is fixed but whose actual pitches are relatively uncertain. Various gradations between this and ordinary singing are found. In the music of the Northwest Coast tribes the recitative characteristics of the pitch movement subside in favor of fairly well established pitches; but the use of one predominant tone as the basis of the song as well as the asymmetrical rhythmic organization serve to preserve its recitative-like character.

The Eskimo-Northwest Coast area is divided into three sub-areas: the Eskimo, the Salish, and the Northwest Coast tribes, and are discussed in that order.

The musical style of the Eskimo has been summarized in a recent monograph by Estreicher,[11] who includes transcriptions of 47 songs. The same author has also treated the music of the Caribou Eskimo separately.[12] The most important collections of Eskimo melodies were published in the first quarter of the twentieth

---

[10] Roberts, 1936, p. 30.

[11] Zygmunt Estreicher, "Die Musik der Eskimos," *Anthropos,* **45** (1950), 659–720.

[12] Estreicher, "La Musique des Esquimaux-Caribou," *Bulletin de la Société Neuchâteloise de Géographie,* **54** (1948), 1–54.

century and earlier. Roberts and Jenness[13] have published material on the Copper Eskimo. Boas[14] has published transcriptions (made by himself and J. C. Fillmore) of Central Eskimo music, and Thuren and Thalbitzer[15] have contributed material on Greenland Eskimo music.

The range of Eskimo songs is restricted; it is seldom greater than an octave and averages between a fifth and a major sixth. The scales are predominantly pentatonic, tetratonic, and tritonic; these three types, about equally distributed, account for over 95 per cent of the material. The intervals of the scales are primarily major seconds and minor thirds. Some minor seconds, major thirds, and a few perfect fourths are also found.

The melodic movement tends to be undulating with about equal amounts of ascent and descent. Towards the end of the song, there is usually descent. The melodies move mainly in seconds and thirds. In the music of the Greenland Eskimo, where tonometric measurements were made, Thuren and Thalbitzer found 5/4 and 3/4 tones and neutral thirds as common as other intervals. Because of the recitative-like quality of many Eskimo songs, many of the pitches in the scales are uncertain. In some songs there are both certain and uncertain pitches (e.g. Thalbitzer Nos. 2 and 4). The use of a series of tones with the same pitch is common in Eskimo music (Thalbitzer Nos. 17 and 33) and the use of recitative alternated with ordinary singing is also found (Thalbitzer Nos. 67, 69).

The rhythm of Eskimo music is relatively complex compared to the other aspects of the style. Both Thuren and Roberts note the Eskimos' sense of rhythmic subtlety. The general rhythmic picture is one of asymmetry and variety. Many songs are dominated by only a few, perhaps two, durational values; many others show diversity by having great contrasts between very long and very short tones. Again, we find successions of tones with the same note value and also much contrast in the alternating use of several values. Dotted rhythms and syncopation are common.

Most of the Eskimo songs cannot be easily classified as metric at all. They often consist of sequences of rhythmic values which defy organization at a level lower than sectional. If the material is divided into meter-like units on the basis of melodic contours, these units are of varying length within each song; they are organized heterometrically; isorhythmic organization is absent. However, the lack of metric organization should not be interpreted to mean rhythmic freedom in performance. The rhythmic material of a song is fixed; it is performed in the same way in each rendition of the song and by each group of singers.

There is instrumental accompaniment to most of the songs: it consists of rhythmic beating of a drum or a part of the human body, and is supplemented by body movements. Its rhythms are relatively complex compared to most of the North American material and are related to those used in the accompaniment of the Northwest Coast tribes. The tempo of Eskimo music is relatively slow compared to most of the continent.

The forms of Eskimo music vary. About half of them could be classified as progressive while among the others a great deal of iteration and variation occurs.

[13] Helen H. Roberts and Diamond Jenness, *Songs of the Copper Eskimo* (Ottawa, 1925).
[14] Franz Boas, *The Central Eskimo* (Washington, 1888).
[15] Hjalmar Thuren and William Thalbitzer, *The Eskimo Music* (Copenhagen, 1911).

Many songs cannot easily be divided into sections (e.g. Thalbitzer Nos. 114, 118). Most of them do share one characteristic trait: that of variation and repetition of short motifs. Even in the progressive forms, different versions of the same motif recur at various points. Sometimes these motifs are long enough to be called phrases or sections: in that case, forms like the following are found: A^1 B C A^2 B C A^3 B C A^4 B C A^5 B (Thalbitzer No. 81).

The songs of the Eskimo are sometimes strophic and more often throughcomposed (in contrast to progressive). While the designation of progressive refers only to a single strophe, the designation of throughcomposed refers to an entire song. The sub-division of the strophic songs is often made on the basis of responsorial technique; Thuren describes the alternation of solo and chorus in Greenland, where the refrain is usually more fixed than the verse strophe. The use of recitative before, during, and after a melody is common. There appears to be no marked tendency for longer sections to appear towards the end of a song, a tendency common in much folk and primitive music.

The vocal technique of the Eskimo approximates that of many North American tribes, particularly those of the Plains-Pueblo musical area. There is a good deal of vocal tension and rhythmic pulsation on the longer tones (a technique described in more detail in Section 6, below). Accents and rests are common, as are stressed grace notes (appoggiaturas). However, this type of vocal technique is not used with such intensity here as it is in the Pueblo-Plains area, although it is definitely present.

Estreicher has succeeded in reconstructing tentatively the historic development of Eskimo music. He finds three stages to be the main points of this development. The first is represented by the music of the Caribou Eskimo, whose style is the simplest. This was superseded by the influences of American Indian and Paleo-Siberian styles which are today found primarily in Alaska and Greenland. The last stage is a development in Eskimo music possibly initiated by the Copper Eskimo, and which has settled primarily in Alaska. The Caribou Eskimo have remained aloof from these latter two stages.

The remainder of the Eskimo-Northwest Coast area is divided into two sub-areas, mainly on the basis of complexity. A simpler style prevails among the Salish tribes while the more complex cultures, such as the Kwakiutl, Nootka, and Tsimshian, participate in a more complex variety of the style. Material on individual tribal styles has been published by Stumpf,[16] (who includes nine transcriptions) Herzog[17] (18 songs), Roberts and Haeberlin,[18] (16 songs) and Abraham and Hornbostel[19] (44 songs), the largest and best study. Material from a number of different tribes in British Columbia which are not accurately identified has been

[16] Carl Stumpf, "Lieder der Bellakula Indianer," *Vierteljahrschrift für Musikwissenschaft,* **2** (1886), 504–526.

[17] Herzog, "Appendix: Songs," in Thelma Adamson, *Folk Tales of the Coast Salish* (Memoirs of the American Folk-Lore Society), **27** (1934), 422–430.

[18] Helen H. Roberts and Herman K. Haeberlin, "Some Songs of the Puget Sound Salish," *JAF,* **31** (1918), 496–520.

[19] Otto Abraham and E. M. von Hornbostel, "Phonographierte Indianermelodien aus British Columbia," in *Boas Anniversary Volume* (New York, 1906), 447–474.

published by Densmore,[20] who includes transcriptions of 98 songs. The main features of the Salish style have been described by Herzog[21] in a study without musical examples. The area as a whole may be said to be relatively well documented, but large groups of transcriptions from individual tribes are as yet lacking.

The range of Salish songs is relatively small; the average is about a major sixth. A number of songs do, however, exhibit ranges larger than an octave. The scales are most frequently pentatonic; hexatonic and tetratonic scales are also very common. The intervals in the scales are most frequently major and minor seconds, and minor thirds. Minor seconds appear more frequently here than in North American Indian music in general. The melodic contours are usually undulating or level; this is true especially of the melodies with small range. In melodies of larger ambitus the movement could be described as pendulum-like, moving in broad jumps from one extreme of the range to the other. The main intervals of the Salish melodies are major and minor thirds. However, their proportion to the total material is not as great as it is in the other musical areas. In Salish music there are more major thirds and perfect fourths on the one hand, and more minor seconds on the other, than elsewhere on the continent. Successions of thirds, or of a third and a fourth (triad-like melodic movement) moving in the same direction are common in Salish music.

The rhythm of Salish music is dominated by several durational values; three or four is most common. This contrasts with Eskimo music, where more are usually found, and with the music of the Athabascan (and some other) musical areas, where less values are common. In contrast to Eskimo music, a rather large proportion (over 50 per cent) of the songs are either entirely or predominantly isometric. Triplets juxtaposed to duplets and dotted rhythms are common. Isorhythmic construction is very rare. Rhythms based on ternary division are common, as are units of five and seven beats; the latter is rare elsewhere on the continent. The final tones of the songs are usually long.

The relationship between the melody and the rhythmic accompaniment is often intricate. It may be syncopated and the rates of speed of the two rhythms may differ. The beating is not usually in a regular pulse but is likely to have a rhythmic design of its own.

The forms of the Salish songs are both strophic and throughcomposed. They may be characterized by a certain lack of clarity and by looseness which is not found in the other musical areas. The main formal principles involved are progression and iteration. The use of variation in the iterative material is frequent. The repeated use of a short motif in basically progressive material is also found. Examples of this characteristic looseness are found in Hornbostel and Abraham: A¹ A² A³ B C¹ C² D¹ D² (No. 9); A¹ B¹ B² B³ B⁴ A² A³ (No. 8).

The use of recitative-like performance of some songs, as well as the alternation of ordinary singing with recitative, are described by Abraham and Hornbostel. The Salish songs are of the average length of North American Indian songs; some-

[20] Frances Densmore, *Music of the Indians of British Columbia* (Anthropological Papers, 27, Bulletin 136 of the Bureau of American Ethnology, Washington, 1943).

[21] Herzog, "Salish Music," in Marian W. Smith, ed., *Indians of the Urban Northwest* (New York, 1949), 93–110.

what less than a minute for a strophe is common. The tempo is somewhat slower than that of the Northwest Coast tribes. The number of phrases or sections in a song is relatively large, averaging between six and twelve.

Herzog mentions a number of examples of polyphony, or part-singing, among the Salish, some of which he attributes to possible accident. Most of them are of the drone type: a single tone is held while another voice produces a moving melody. One example places the drone tone a fifth below the tonic of the melody. Since the use of repeated tones is common in the Salish style, the accompaniment of such a section by a monotone could more easily be ascribed to accident than the use of a drone against a moving melody. However, the number of instances reported indicates at least a slight development of polyphony in this musical sub-area; it is probably totally absent in most of the other musical areas of North America.

The vocal technique of the Salish is comparable to that of the Eskimo. Vocal tension, comparable to that produced by what is considered improper singing of high tones in Western culture, and pulsations on the longer tones are found to a moderate degree, but to one less intense than that of the Plains-Pueblo area.

The rather complex style of the Northwest Coast tribes is shared by the Kwakiutl, Tsimshian, Nootka, Makah, and Quileute. Forty-six Kwakiutl (including a few Nootka) songs were transcribed by Boas and Fillmore.[22] Two hundred ten songs of the Makah, Quileute, and Nootka were published by Densmore.[23] Seventy-five melodies of the Tsimshian, with some notes, were published by Barbeau.[24] This material was supplemented by the writer's aural analysis which corroborated the findings based on published transcriptions.

The ranges of Northwest Coast songs are usually somewhat wider than those of Eskimo and Salish; however, they still are restricted in comparison with those of other musical areas. The average is slightly over a major sixth. Ranges of a major sixth, perfect fifth, and perfect octave are the most common. The Tsimshian have a slightly larger average, major seventh.

Pentatonic scales are the most common, accounting for about 40 per cent of the published material. Next in frequency are tetratonic scales followed by approximately equal distribution of hexatonic and tritonic scales. The intervals of the scales are the same as those of Salish music: minor seconds and major thirds are more common here than in the other musical areas. Tritonic scales, common especially among the Tsimshian, are usually made up of some kind of triad-like formation. The tonic is the lowest tone in about half of the songs.

The melodic movement is usually undulating; descent outweighs ascent, however. About 55 per cent of the melodic progressions are downward. The melodic intervals tend to be large (major thirds, perfect fourths, perfect and diminished fifths) on the one hand, and small (minor seconds) on the other. Major seconds

[22] Boas, *The Social Organization and the Secret Societies of the Kwakiutl Indians* (Washington, 1897).

[23] Densmore, *Nootka and Quileute Music* (Bulletin 124 of the Bureau of American Ethnology, Washington, 1939).

[24] Garfield, Wingert, and Barbeau, *The Tsimshian: their Arts and Music* (Publications of the American Ethnological Society, 18, New York, 1952).

and minor thirds do not predominate to the extent they do in other areas. The tendency to progress rapidly from one limit of the range to the other is found here, as in the Salish style.

The rhythm of Northwest Coast songs is dominated by three or four durational values. Some melodies are dominated by only two. Contrast between very long and very short values is common, as are the use of triplets, syncopation, and series of tones with the same durational value. Recitative-like rhythmic complexity is found; this is often correlated with uncertain pitches to produce recitative effects similar to those of Eskimo music but different from the song-recitative of the Great Basin musical area.

Most of the songs are heterometric; metric divisions are sometimes difficult to make. Isorhythmic construction seems absent. The relationship between the rhythmic instrumental accompaniment and the melody is the most complex of the continent. Actual rhythmic polyphony, the simultaneous use of two or more rhythmic structures, is found here. Favorite devices include the use of quintuple meter in the accompaniment together with duple meter in the melody. The tempo of Northwest Coast songs is relatively slow.

The lengths of Northwest Coast songs vary more than those of most musical areas. Some (e.g. Densmore, Nootka, Nos. 18 and 151) are longer than most of the North American ones, while others are exceedingly short (e.g. Densmore, Nootka Nos. 5, 6, and 22). The forms are mostly strophic, although a good deal of variation is allowed among the various strophes of an individual song. The strophes themselves consist of a number of sections, from three to ten, which vary in length; it is not possible to say that they always grow progressively longer, although they sometimes do. The strophes are usually progressive in form, with repetition and variation of motifs fairly common. This is shared with the Salish and Eskimo styles.

Occasionally a type of form, common among the Plains Indians and represented by the letters $A^1 A^2$ (with A^2 shorter than A^1), is found (e.g. Densmore, Nootka Nos. 33 and 40). A type of form common in Central and Southern California, called the Rise, is also found in some songs. It consists of a number of sections which often contain the same material, followed by one higher in pitch; this is again followed by the initial material which closes the song. It is found in about 10 per cent of the total Northwest Coast material and in about 35 per cent of the Tsimshian songs.

The vocal technique of the Northwest Coast approximates that of the Salish. A moderate amount of pulsation and vocal tension is found. Densmore describes a drone type of polyphony among the Quileute where only certain women are considered competent to sing a single long tone above the melody. Antiphonal and responsorial techniques, contrast between singers and between verse and refrain sections in the text, are described by Herzog.

The traits which tie together the styles of the Eskimo, Salish, and Northwest Coast Indians were discussed above. The characteristics by which they are distinguished are summarized here. These are primarily degrees of complexity, particularly in scale, form, and polyphony. While the Eskimo have one of the simplest styles of North America, the Northwest Coast tribes have one of the most complex; the Salish tribes are in an intermediate position. In Northwest Coast music there is primarily an elaboration of the traits already characteristic of Eskimo and Salish music: rhythmic complexity, recitative-like singing, and structural lack of clarity and fixity. This is paralleled by the paucity of musical instruments and song functions of the Eskimo in contrast with the large number of these on the Northwest Coast. Salish style has evidently been influenced by the Northwest Coast in many ways, and it has also had contact, apparently, with the Plains-Pueblo style, some of whose elements appear in it, and to which it is geographically closer than are the Northwest Coast tribes and the Eskimo.

3. The Great Basin Area

Some of the tribes of the Great Basin of Utah and Nevada as well as some in Northern California and Southern Oregon constitute a stylistic unit. The area as a whole is not well documented musically and more material is needed to ascertain its geographic limits. The most important source on Great Basin music is a monograph by Herzog[1][2] which makes some statements about the general nature of the music of the Basin tribes (not including Oregon). Herzog made use of some unpublished transcriptions of Paiute music.[3] Additional source material includes 19 songs of the Owens Valley Paiute published by Steward.[4] A number of songs of the Paiute, Modoc, and Klamath were published by de Angulo and d'Harcourt.[5] The music of the Northern Ute, which is to some extent marginal to this area, has been treated by Densmore,[6] who includes 114 transcriptions. The musical style of the Modoc is described by Hall[7] in a manuscript paper including 20 songs. Finally, the songs of the Ghost Dance, a religious movement which spread over a large part of North America in the late 19th century and which carried with it the musical style of the Basin, is described by Herzog. One hundred and thirty-two songs of the Ghost Dance from several tribes, mainly on the Plains, were published by Mooney[8] in his extensive study on the Ghost Dance. The style of the Ghost Dance songs is related to that of the Great Basin songs.

The general characteristics of the Great Basin musical area show it to be the one with the simplest styles on the continent. These are the use of a small melodic range, lack of much vocal tension and pulsation in the singing, and lack of

[1][2] George Herzog, "Plains Ghost Dance and Great Basin Music," *American Anthropologist,* **37** (1935), 403–419.

[3] Edward Sapir, unpublished manuscript on Southern Paiute music with transcriptions by Jacob D. Sapir.

[4] Julian H. Steward, *Ethnography of the Owens Valley Paiute* (University of California Publications in American Archeology and Anthropology, **33**, Berkeley, 1933), pp. 233–350.

[5] Jaime de Angulo and M. B. d'Harcourt, "La musique des Indiens de la Californie du Nord," *Journal de la Société des Américanistes,* **23** (1931), 189–228.

[6] Frances Densmore, *Northern Ute Music* (Bureau of American Ethnology, Bulletin **75**, Washington, 1922).

[7] Jody C. Hall, *Musical Style of the Modoc,* MS., Indiana University, 1952.

[8] James Mooney, *The Ghost-Dance Religion and the Sioux Outbreak of 1890* (Annual Report of the Bureau of American Ethnology, **14**: 2, Washington, 1896).

specialized melodic movement which consists, rather, of descending, undulating, and arc-shaped progressions. It is in the over-all structure of the songs that the area is best typified. The majority of the songs employ the "paired-phrase" patterns, in which each phrase is repeated. This type of form is found sporadically elsewhere on the continent but it does not characterize the other areas. A further stigma is the tendency for most of the phrases to end on the tonic; this contrasts with most other styles, whose phrase endings tend to fall on different tones with the last one only on the tonic.

The Great Basin musical area consists of a number of sub-styles which are discussed in the following order: Northern California and Southern Oregon, Paiute and Ghost Dance, and Northern Ute. In addition, a style which is widespread throughout North America and which is related to the Great Basin style by virtue of its simplicity and some other features, is discussed in this section. Described by Herzog,[9] it is found in many lullabies, songs from tales, and gambling songs from a number of tribes.

The style of the Modoc and Klamath is among the simplest in North America and of primitive music in general. Among the Modoc there is a large proportion of two-tone and three-tone scales. Only about 40 per cent have four or more tones. The intervals in the ditonic and tritonic scales are almost exclusively major seconds and minor thirds. In the scales with more tones there are, in addition to these intervals, also some minor seconds and a very few major thirds. The range of the songs is also small; more than half have a range of a perfect fourth or less; a range as great as an octave is exceedingly rare.

The melodic movement of Modoc and Klamath music is relatively undulating with a somewhat greater proportion of descent than ascent. The melodic intervals are small; major and minor seconds and minor thirds predominate.

The rhythm of Modoc music is dominated by relatively few durational values with the exception of about 30 per cent of the songs, where four or five are found. About half of the songs are isometric; the rest are heterometric and have a tendency towards recitative-like construction. Final tones tend to be of average or short length. Triplets and dotted rhythms are relatively rare. None of the recorded material has rhythmic accompaniment; thus, no conclusions can be drawn about that phase of the music.

The songs of the Modoc are short. They are strophic, a strophe lasting about 15 seconds. Their forms represent the simplest variety of the paired-phrase patterns characteristic of this area: more than half of them consist of one phrase which is repeated, sometimes with variations. It is possible that the more complex paired-phrase types among the Basin tribes developed from this simple type. Other forms found among the Modoc include: $A^1 A^2 B$ (Hall No. 1); A B A B (Hall No. 3); A B C D (Hall No. 7).

The vocal technique of the Modoc is relatively free of pulsation; occasionally this is found, but never to the same degree as in the Plains-Pueblo area, and even to a lesser extent than in the Eskimo-Northwest Coast material.

Hall divides the Modoc songs into two distinct types, I and II, of which I is

[9] Herzog, "Special Song Types in North American Indian Music," *Zeitschrift für vergleichende Musikwissenschaft,* 3 (1935), 23–33.

the simpler, here summarized—Type I: 1. range of a perfect fourth or less; 2. ditonic or tritonic scales; 3. no tones in the melody lower than the tonic; 4. arc-shaped melodic contour; 5. final intervals move from an important tone to the tonic; 6. rhythmic material has only two durational values and is usually characterized by frequent shifting or contrast of values; 7. isometric construction. Type II: 1. range between a perfect fifth and an octave; 2. gradually descending or undulating melodic contour; 3. scales of four to six tones; 4. little or infrequent contrast between durational values, a full unbroken beat being the basic value; 5. scales include tones higher and lower than the tonic; 6. rhythmic material consists of two or more durational values; 7. isometric or heterometric construction. Type I is typical of Modoc and Klamath music; it is found in the majority of the songs. Type II is more closely related to the music of the Paiutes and the Ghost Dance in melody, scale, and rhythmic construction, but not in form.

The style of the Great Basin proper, i.e., the Paiutes, and that of the Ghost Dance songs of the central portion of North America, although akin to Type II of the Modoc, also shows relationships to Type I. The range of the songs is usually between a perfect fifth and an octave. The scales are pentatonic and tetratonic; tritonic and hexatonic scales are rare. The intervals of the scales are predominantly major and minor seconds. Minor thirds do occur but major thirds are rare. The scale construction is basically diatonic; the lowest interval is likely to be larger than a second. The tonic is usually the lowest tone and the other important tones are immediately above the tonic.

The melodic movement is often gradually descending and very rarely of the terrace variety common in the Plains-Pueblo musical area. Individual phrases are likely to be of descending, arc, and undulating types of movement. The same intervals found in the scales are used in the melodies; diatonic progressions are common.

The rhythm of Paiute and Ghost Dance music is dominated by three or four durational values. The organization is only rarely isometric, and the metric units tend to become longer as a song progresses. However, the single repetition of a metric unit is common; this is in line with the paired-phrase structure.

Information on the percussive accompaniment of songs is scanty. However, it may be safely assumed that the use of instrumental accompaniment is by no means as widespread in this area as among most North American tribes. Most of the Ghost Dance songs on the Plains are also sung without rhythmic accompaniment. The tempo of the Basin songs varies; it averages about the same as most North American music and is slightly faster than that of the Eskimo-Northwest Coast area.

The songs of the Great Basin area are usually strophic, a strophe lasting about 45 seconds. The phrases are of varying lengths; some consist of only four or five tones while others take up 20 or more. Phrases of considerably varying lengths are found within the same song. The forms often adhere to the paired-phrase principle. Here are some examples of the most common kinds: A A B B (Mooney No. 45); A A B B C C (Mooney, p. 965); A^1 A^2 B B C C A^1 A^2 D D E E (Densmore, Pawnee, p. 57). Sometimes a group of two phrases is used as the unit of repetition: A A B C B C (Herzog, p. 410). In most songs which do not adhere rigidly to the paired-phrase principle the iterative elements still predominate: A B C D D E E (Herzog, p. 407). In a few songs the iterative element appears more strongly yet; a section is repeated more than once and also varied: A A B¹ B¹ B² B² C C (Mooney, p. 1096). A number of songs exhibit other kinds of forms which may be designated as reverting and progressive.

The characteristic phrase-ending on the tonic, described in the introductory portion of this section, is found in Paiute and Ghost Dance songs. Roughly 80 per cent of all phrases end on the tonic.

The vocal technique of the Paiute and Ghost Dance songs is generally free of pulsation and vocal tension and is roughly comparable to that used in most Western European folk music. This is true even in those Ghost Dance songs which are performed by tribes whose general style of singing contains pulsation and vocal tension, such as those of the Plains.

The music of the Northern Ute is generally a mixture of songs in the Great Basin style with some in the style of the Plains. About one-third of their songs may be classified as belonging strictly to the Basin style; the rest either approximate the style of the Plains-Pueblo area or are of mixed style. Among the songs in the Great Basin style, those of the Bear Dance are most prominent. Their chief deviation from the style of the Paiute and Ghost Dance songs consists of the use of slightly larger range (averaging a major sixth to an octave) and somewhat more complex rhythmic construction. The latter is due primarily to the use of more durational values. In over-all form and phrase endings, as well as in melodic movement, these Northern Ute songs adhere to the general Great Basin pattern.

Most of the Northern Ute songs have instrumental accompaniment: this is often drumming and occasionally with the use of a notched stick idiophone. The rhythm is usually a simple pulse, but triplets with one unit as a rest as well as tremolo alternating with pulse beating are also found. In general, these rhythms are similar to those used in the Plains accompaniments.

A type of song which has rarely been recorded but which seems to be characteristic of the Great Basin tribes is a kind which in itself narrates a myth; it is one of the few examples of narrative songs in primitive cultures. Described by Sapir,[10] its style is similar to that of the Great Basin in melody and rhythm, but its form is basically progressive. Short motifs, however, may be repeated and varied. Densmore offers two such songs, calling them "rudimentary songs," which fit in with Sapir's description. Their medolic movement is gradually descending, with much interposed ascent. The rhythmic structure is complex, heterometric, and in general rather free. The song texts narrate entire animal tales. Densmore indicates that they may have been performed with drum accompaniment, but she does not record it.

Three song types which are found in many North American Indian tribes of several culture and musical areas should be included here. Described by Herzog,[11] they exhibit general similarity to the songs of the Great Basin musical area, especially those of the Modoc. Some other tribes in which they have been recorded

[10] Edward Sapir, "Song Recitative in Paiute Mythology," *JAF,* **23** (1910), 455–472.
[11] Herzog, "Special Song Types in North American Indian Music," 23–33.

are the Clackamas, Ute, Dakota, Menomini, Winnebago, Tonkawa, Arapaho, and Shawnee.

The first type of this group is connected with animal tales. It is characterized by its adherence to speech-melody and its recitative-like performance. The second, connected with gambling and hiding games, is characterized by short phrases which are sometimes repeated in the paired-phrase manner of the Great Basin style. A third, consisting of lullabies, is characterized by especially small range (seconds and thirds) and by iterative elements in the form. All of them share the use of few tones in the scale, undulating melodic movement, and extreme brevity (10 to 20 seconds). It should be emphasized that not all gambling songs, songs from tales, and lullabies have these features; many do not. But the traits described above are usually, when they are present outside the Great Basin musical area, connected with the mentioned song functions. Herzog believes these types to be archaic layers in Indian music. Their relationship to Great Basin music is by virtue of their simplicity rather than many concrete features. It is possible that both styles can be shown to be archaic, and both may go back to one very simple style which has disappeared. More comparative study of these styles could give some insight into the early stages of North American Indian music.

4. The California-Yuman Area

This area includes the major part of aboriginal California and the Yuman language family. The music of Central California has been studied by Abraham[12] (including the Pomo, Miwok, Patwin, and Maidu). Some of the tribes of Southern California (Luiseño, Gabrielino, and Catalineño) have been treated by Roberts[13] who includes 27 transcriptions. Herzog[14] has described the music of the Yuman tribes (Mohave, Yuma, Diegueno, Maricopa, and Yavapai); his study includes 39 songs. Seven additional songs of the Maricopa, transcribed by Herzog appear in a work by Spier.[15] One hundred and thirty songs of the Yuma, Cocopa, and Yaqui have been published by Densmore.[16] About 25 California Indian songs belonging to tribes in this musical area are included in a study by de Angulo and d'Harcourt;[17] the tribes included here are the Pomo, Miwok, Karok, and Maidu. Some of the tribes of Northern California (e.g., Klamath) are not included in this area and were discussed in Section 3. The total number of transcriptions for this area is not large, but descriptions of the styles have been written by well-trained scholars; they have been supplemented by aural analysis by the writer.

The California-Yuman area is characterized by two important traits: the use of a relaxed, non-pulsating vocal technique, which is found here to a greater degree than elsewhere on the continent, including even the Great Basin musical area, and

[12] Peter F. Abraham, personal communication to the writer, January 1953.

[13] Helen H. Roberts, *Form in Primitive Music* (New York, 1933).

[14] Herzog, "The Yuman Musical Style," *JAF*, 41 (1928), 183–231.

[15] Herzog, "Maricopa Music," in Leslie Spier, *The Yuman Tribes of the Gila River* (Chicago, 1933), 271–279.

[16] Densmore, *Yuman and Yaqui Music* (Bureau of American Ethnology, Bulletin 110, Washington, 1932).

[17] de Angulo and d'Harcourt, 1931, 189–228.

the presence of the Rise, a type of form and melodic movement. The latter is characteristic of the California-Yuman area, and, while it is found in some songs of other areas, is found in the majority of the songs here. The Rise consists of the interruption of the general melodic trend, which is usually the repetition of a short section or at least movement in a restricted range, by material with higher pitches. It is described by Herzog:

In the introduced parts the melody turns upward. This 'rise' in the melody is decidedly peculiar to Yuman music. The higher part may repeat part of the main motif. In some of the gambling songs the higher part is a partial repetition of the motif in the higher octave. More commonly the higher part is an imitation of part of the main motif. Or, the higher part may shift the melodic balance higher, by tones which were not employed in the song before.[18]

The description of the style in the next several paragraphs applies mainly to the Yuman tribes and those of Southern California. The Central Californian tribes share in the style, and their deviations from it are mentioned below. The range of the songs tends to be relatively small; the average is between a fifth and a major ninth. Separate sections of a song are often even more restricted in range. The Rise section and the rest of the song may occupy different pitch levels, and each portion may have only a small range (third or fifth), while the combination of the two, the total tonal material of a song, has a larger ambitus.

The scales of the songs in this area are primarily pentatonic; next in frequency are tetratonic scales. The intervals in the scales are mainly major seconds and minor thirds, but major thirds are relatively common. The tonic is the lowest tone in about 60 per cent of the scales and is otherwise also near the bottom of the range. Other important tones are usually above the tonic at distances of a major third, a perfect fourth, or a perfect fifth from it.

The melodic movement (not considering the basic contrast between the Rise and the remaining portion of a song) is most often descending but not of the terrace variety found in the Plains-Pueblo area. About one-third of it is not descending, however, but is either level or undulating and sometimes arc-shaped, with balanced upward and downward movement, the descent in final position. Of the total melodic progressions (intervals), about 45 per cent are ascending. The melodic intervals are mainly major and minor seconds and minor thirds. Major thirds, perfect fourths, and perfect fifths are also relatively common, as are octaves, which occur between the non-Rise and the Rise portions of a song. Other large intervals are rare.

The Rise usually consists of the introduction of higher tones than previously found in the song. This is not always true, however, for in some songs the general level of pitch rises without new tones being introduced into the scale. In two of the songs published by Roberts (Nos. 10 and 11) there is actually a drop in pitch level rather than a Rise.

Melodic sequences, transposition of motifs to small intervals like seconds and thirds, are a feature of Southern Californian music. These contrast, because of the small intervals of transposition, with the sequences found in the Plains-Pueblo

[18] Herzog, 1928, 193.

musical area which are usually at distances of fourths and fifths and could perhaps be designated as imitation rather than sequence.

The rhythm of Yuman and Southern Californian songs is dominated by about three durational values. Syncopation is common, but is sung with less stress on the first two notes than the same figure would be in the Plains-Pueblo area. Dotted rhythms are moderately frequent; triplets are rather common. The final tones of songs are about equally distributed among long, average, and short durational values. Isometric organization is somewhat more common in this area than elsewhere on the continent (with isolated exceptions, such as the Salish and the Southeastern U. S.), but it is not found in the majority of the songs. This may be due to a tendency towards isorhythmic organization which is not found consistently throughout a song, but which may be present in individual sections of songs. Complex meters such as five-eighths are found occasionally.

The rhythmic accompaniment of Yuman and Southern Californian songs is used both for introducing and closing a song as well as during the melody. While singing is in progress, the accompaniment is usually the same tempo as the singing, but it may execute different figures and designs. This is more complex than the melody-accompaniment relationship in all of the other musical areas with the exception of the Eskimo-Northwest Coast. The accompaniment rests at points of rest in the melody. During the Rise portion the rhythmic accompaniment usually contrasts with that of the remainder of the song; tremolo is often found at this point.

The forms of the Yuman and Californian songs must be considered a combination of strophic and throughcomposed (but not progressive) principles. Its outstanding feature is the Rise, the material surrounding it being varied. Among the Yumans, the non-Rise portion of a song usually consists of one section which is repeated several times, the number of repetitions apparently being arbitrary. Thus each song is not always sung the same way and the entire song cannot easily be considered a strophe unless much leeway is assumed. It might perhaps be possible to consider each occurrence of the non-Rise motif as one strophe; this type of analysis is supported by the fact that in some songs the Rise portion is merely an octave transposition of the non-Rise portion. The song could then be considered strophic, with a short strophe as the basic unit. However, for songs in which the non-Rise portion is not merely iterative this analysis is not adequate. It is perhaps best to consider the form as one which does not fit into either the strophic or the throughcomposed categories. The most important principle of the forms, besides the Rise, is that of iteration. This is especially true of the Yuman songs, while among the Southern Californian ones the non-Rise portion tends to be more complex and to employ the progressive and reverting principles. Nos. 8 and 9 of Roberts' collection indicate somewhat greater complexity of form than is found elsewhere in the area, but the Rise is still present.

Following are some examples of forms among the Yumans. They are the most common ones of the area: A A A . . . Rise A (Herzog, Yuman, 1, 20, 25, 34); A B A B A B . . . Rise B (Herzog, Yuman, 7, 27, 33); A B A B . . . A Rise B (Herzog, Yuman, 4, 23). Around the Rise portion a curtailment of the non-Rise repeated section is sometimes found: A B A B . . . Rise A^2 B (Herzog, Yuman, 6,

28). The number of repetitions of the non-Rise portion is usually, as indicated, arbitrary. Each section (indicated by one letter in the examples) of a song consists of between one and four phrases. These are usually of about equal length and consist of from five to twelve notes. The songs themselves (the entire rendition) are about a minute in length.

The vocal technique of Southern Californian and Yuman music is comparable to that of most Western European folk singing. Songs are often concluded by rhythmic shouting; some song series have their own characteristic shouts which are used to close each song. The use of rhythmic grunting and shouting as a type of percussive-like accompaniment to melodies is found occasionally.

Two flute melodies of the Yuma are offered by Densmore. These have a range of a minor third and a major third, respectively. The melodies are primarily progressive, but the repeated use of the same short motifs and intervals ties them together to constitute a kind of rhapsodic form. The flute melodies are ornamented more than the vocal ones. In them one finds greater contrasts between long and short durational values, a large number of durational values, and generally more complex rhythmic organization.

The music of the Central Californian tribes has been studied by Peter F. Abraham, who has communicated his findings to the writer. Aside from a few brief notes, his material is not summarized here, because of its forthcoming independent publication. The Central Californian style is generally similar to that of Southern California and the Yumans. It differs only in two important respects: the amount of rhythmic complexity and the vocal technique found here are not present in the Southern portions of the musical area. Central California has greater rhythmic complexity and tenser vocal technique, but is formally·simpler. The presence of the Rise as well as melodic and tonal considerations make the identification of these two main styles as part of the California-Yuman area necessary.

5. THE ATHABASCAN AREA

The nature of the style of the Athabascan area and the tribes which it includes is more indefinite than corresponding data are for the other musical areas. The writer's present estimate is that the area includes the Navaho and Apache and, possibly, the Northern Athabascans (or at least some of them). Also included in this Section is a discussion of the style of the Peyote songs used mainly on the Great Plains. This style bears similarities to, and may be historically derived from, the style of the Navaho and Apache.

The total number of songs published from the Athabascan area (exclusive of Peyote songs) scarcely exceeds 50. This is somewhat unexpected in view of the fact that more songs have been recorded among the Navaho than in any other single North American tribe. Eleven Navaho songs were published by Matthews;[19] they were transcribed by Fillmore. Twelve were published by Curtis-Burlin [20] and

[19] Washington Matthews, *Navaho Legends* (Memoirs of the American Folk-Lore Society, 5, New York, 1897).
[20] Natalie Curtis-Burlin, *The Indians' Book* (New York and London, 1907).

six by Herzog.[21] Transcriptions of Apache songs are even scarcer. Curtis-Burlin[22] has printed seven and Roberts[23] two. Published transcriptions of Northern Athabascan songs are rarer yet. Two songs (probably Tahltan), with considerable comment, were published by Barbeau,[24] and Roberts[25] makes a few descriptive statements comparing the style with that of the Navaho. It must be especially emphasized that statements made about the constituency and style of the Athabascan area as a whole are highly tentative. It should also be understood that the area is not contiguous as are the others. It is made up primarily of the members of one large language family distributed in two large segments over the Western part of the continent. Only the Southern segment is known to an adequate degree. The Northern part is almost unknown and is the weakest link in the North American Indian material available for study. The entire discussion of the Athabascan area is therefore brief.

The distinguishing marks of the Athabascan area are the use of few (usually two) durational values, a large number of arc-shaped melodic contours, and the predominant use of relatively large intervals (thirds, fourths, fifths, sixths, and octaves) in the melody, with scarcity of seconds.

The average range of Navaho and Apache songs is about an octave, but there is considerable variety; some have ranges as large as two octaves. The range of Navaho songs is greater than that of the other tribes in this musical area. The scales are mostly pentatonic and tetratonic; some tritonic ones are found, usually in triad-like formations. The intervals of the scales are mostly major and minor thirds, major seconds, and perfect fourths. The tonic is usually the lowest tone in the range, occasionally a tone above the lowest. In the latter case, the lowest tone is usually a perfect fourth below the tonic. Other important tones in the scales tend to be perfect fifths and thirds (major, minor, or neutral) above the tonic.

As stated above, the melodic movement tends to be in arc-shaped contours which ascend rapidly and descend somewhat more gradually. The melodic intervals are large; the use of major thirds is more prominent here than in the other areas. Descending and undulating melodic movement is also found; this may be the result of influences from the Great Plains, which are present also in other aspects of the music. The usual tendency is, however, for the melody to move in broad arcs between the upper and lower limits of the range in leaps which approach acrobatic vocal maneuvers. Jumps of an octave are not rare. Flattening of the melody resulting in the repetition of a single pitch at the end of a song is common.

The rhythm of Navaho and Apache music is dominated by two durational values. These are usually related in the ratio 1 to 2, occasionally 1 to 3. Other rhythmic values are used rather rarely, perhaps once or twice during a song, if at all. There is a tendency towards isometric organization. Although completely isometric songs seem to be rare, there are sections using only one meter which is

[21] Herzog, "Speech-Melody and Primitive Music," *Musical Quarterly,* 20 (1934), 452–466.
[22] Curtis-Burlin, 1907.
[23] Roberts, "Indian Music of the Southwest," *Natural History,* 27 (1927), 257–265.
[24] Marius Barbeau, "Songs of the Northwest," *Musical Quarterly,* 19 (1933), 101–111.
[25] Roberts, *Musical Areas in Aboriginal North America* (Yale University Publications in Anthropology, 12, New Haven, 1936), 33.

usually duple or triple but not complex. Change of tempo is not found during a song. Dotted rhythms and triplets (constrasting with duplets) are rare. Final tones are usually short. Some isorhythmic sections are found within some songs, but entire songs with one repeated rhythmic pattern are not found.

The rhythmic accompaniment of the songs is usually in even pulsating beats. These usually correspond to the shorter of the dominant rhythmic values and follow the melody rather closely throughout a song.

The forms of Navaho songs are strophic; a strophe lasts about thirty seconds and consists of three or four sections. The forms show no specialized development comparable to the Rise of the California-Yuman area. Some of the forms have the incomplete repetition type of form ($A^1 A^2$) of the Plains-Pueblo area. Some forms are reverting, others progressive, while others again display iterative tendencies, with repeated sections (e.g., Matthew No. 10). The use of introductory and closing formulae is common; these are usually a number of repeated tones on the tonic pitch. One type of form which cannot be considered strophic without some qualification consists of the alternation of two sections which closes with the first of the two (e.g., A B A B A B A). In general, the phrases towards the end of a song are longer than the initial ones.

The vocal technique of the Navaho and Apache makes use of vocal tension and pulsation to an extent greater than the Eskimo-Northwest Coast area, but with less intensity than the Plains-Pueblo area. The pulsations usually coincide with the basic rhythmic pulse of the song, and they do not give rise to the amount of ornamentation found on the Plains. Falsetto singing is common, but it contrasts with the type of falsetto of the Plains in that it is not accompanied by the violent changes in dynamics, the heavy stresses, and the ornaments of the latter.

The music of the Athabascan tribes in the interior of Canada is almost unknown. Roberts finds it somewhat comparable to that of the Navaho. A few Cree Indian songs exhibit some similarities to Navaho music, particularly in the rhythm (but they are not Athabascan). The Tahltan melodies recorded by Barbeau are similar in style to the Eskimo-Northwest Coast area. On the other hand, some Kutchin and other Northern Athabascan melodies heard by the writer exhibit features in common with Navaho and Apache music. The Northern Athabascans, though apparently in the same musical area as the Southern Athabascans, seem to have been influenced also by Northwest Coast and Plains music, while the Navaho and Apache have taken on, in recent times, some stylistic traits of the Plains-Pueblo musical area and perhaps some from the Great Basin.

The songs of the Peyote cult, which within the last two centuries have spread to many tribes of North America, particularly those in the United States, are related, in musical style, to those of the Navaho and Apache. This may be due to the fact that the style could have spread to these tribes from the Lipan Apache who were the first tribe north of Mexico to use the Peyote buttons for ritual purposes. Today Peyote songs are very large in number and are being composed by members of many tribes. It is possible that, along with the ritual, the style of the songs, and perhaps even some actual songs, were transmitted from the Apache to the various tribes in the United States who use Peyote.

The songs of the Peyote cult differ stylistically from the other songs of their users. They exhibit a stylistic homogeneity which cuts across the boundaries of musical and cultural areas. McAllester[26] has described the Peyote style; his findings are corroborated by those of the writer among the Shawnee and Arapaho.[27] McAllester summarizes the characteristics of the Peyote style: they are sung with relatively "mild" vocal technique; they are fast, and the accompaniment is in quick rhythmic values, corresponding to the faster ones of the melody; they use only two durational values; they have the usual Plains melodic contours, but restricted range and unusually long and monotonic codas; the tonic is the usual phrase final; finally, most Peyote songs end with the meaningless syllable sequence *he ne ne yo wa* or a variant of it.

In general, this picture is that of Navaho and Apache music along with some elements of Plains music, perhaps some of the Great Basin style. The melodic movement is indicative of Plains influence, while the use of paired-phrase patterns is probably an importation from the Great Basin. If the conjectures as to the origin of the Peyote style given here are correct, it offers one of the best examples of the possibility of reconstructing the music history of primitive cultures.

6. The Plains-Pueblo Area

The area whose music is best known and best documented includes the Pueblos, the Plains tribes, the Prairie tribes, and a group of Woodlands tribes around the Western part of the Great Lakes. It is this area the musical style of which was once thought to be the general style of North American Indian music, because the material from it was much more abundant than from the other areas. The characteristics which are common to all parts of this area are also found elsewhere, but it is only in the Plains-Pueblo area that they are all present in the majority of the songs. The size of the area, as well as the amount of available material, makes it possible to delimit a number of sub-areas whose styles differ significantly. These are discussed separately and only those stylistic features which are common to the entire area are given in the next three paragraphs.

The vocal technique of the Plains-Pueblo area was considered by Hornbostel to be racially inherent among all Indians, since it is found also in South America. It is characterized by a great deal of tension in the vocal organs which is sustained throughout a song, an effort to sing as loudly as possible, and pulsation on the longer tones. Strong accents, glissandos, and, as a result, intonation which is probably less stable or fixed than that of the other musical areas, as well as ornamentation and shouting before, during, and after songs are the main results of this tension. This type of singing reaches its greatest intensity in this area, although it is found elsewhere also.

The melodic movement is also distinctive. It is primarily descending. Melodies show the following phrase pattern: each phrase descends, and each begins somewhat lower than the previous one. Towards the end of a song the phrases do not usually descend as much as at the beginning, but they tend to flatten out, as it

[26] David P. McAllester, *Peyote Music* (Viking Fund Publications in Anthropology, 13, New York, 1949).
[27] Bruno Nettl, "Observations on Meaningless Peyote Song Texts," *JAF*, 66 (1953), 161–164.

were, the last phrase lingering on the final, lowest pitch for several notes. Frequently all of these descending phrases have the same, or similar, melodic contours, and may be simply transpositions of the initial phrase. This type of melodic movement as a whole is called the "terrace-type" because of its visual resemblance to terraces in its graphic expression.

The forms of the Plains-Pueblo area are strophic. A strophe consists of five to eight sections or phrases which tend to become longer towards the end of the strophe. One important type of form within this framework, found in the majority of the songs, consists essentially of one long section, of between three and five phrases, which is repeated with the beginning omitted. The main manifestation of this type has been represented by the letters $A^1 A^2$ (in detail, a typical manifestation is A B C, B C). Another important kind of form in this area, also reflecting the principle of incomplete repetition but with the initial part curtailed is represented by $A^1 A^2 B$.

In the following portions of this Section, the musical style of each sub-area is described in some detail. Of these there are four: the Chippewa and Menomini, the Southern Prairies, the typical Plains tribes, and the Pueblos. In addition, the Pima-Papago style is marginal to the area. The tribal repertories as a whole are discussed with the exception of Ghost Dance and Peyote songs, which were recent importations, and lullabies, gambling songs, and songs from tales, which are in the Great Basin style and form an evidently archaic layer on the Plains.

The easternmost sub-area is that represented by the Chippewa [1][2] and Menomini[3] whose music has been collected and transcribed by Densmore in great quantities. A total of 500 songs are available in her publications. The range of most of the Chippewa and Menomini songs is very large; the average is the largest in North America. Of the Chippewa songs, only 9 per cent have a range smaller than an octave and 36 per cent greater than a perfect eleventh. The Menomini ranges are only slightly smaller. In spite of this high average, none of the songs analyzed has a range as large as two octaves, which is found among the Navaho and Pawnee.

The scales of Chippewa and Menomini songs are primarily pentatonic and tetratonic; slightly over half are pentatonic. A small number of tritonic, hexatonic, and heptatonic scales are also found. The scales consist primarily of major seconds and minor thirds they are anhemitonic (without half-tones). Next in frequency are major thirds and perfect fourths. The tonic of a scale is usually the lowest tone, occasionally the next-to-lowest. Tones next to the tonic in importance are often a minor third or a perfect fourth, and occasionally a major second above it.

The melodic movement is almost exclusively of the terrace type. A few songs exhibit a single descending contour. Undulating and arc-shaped contours are rare. The melodic interval progressions are about 65 per cent downward and 35 per cent upward. Melodic intervals are primarily major seconds (50 per cent), minor thirds (27 per cent), and, with much less frequency, minor seconds, major thirds,

[1][2] Frances Densmore, *Chippewa Music* and *Chippewa Music II* (Bureau of American Ethnology, Bulletins 45 and 53, Washington, 1910, 1913).

[3] Densmore, *Menomini Music* (Bureau of American Ethnology, Bulletin 102, Washington, 1913).

perfect fourths, and perfect fifths. The final interval in a song tends to be a major or minor third, occasionally also a major second or perfect fourth.

The rhythm of Chippewa and Menomini songs is relatively complex. Most of the songs are dominated by two or three durational values with some others also present. If there are three main values they are usually in the proportion 1 to 2 to 4. Triplets are common, as are dotted rhythms with the longer note first. A series of notes with the same rhythmic value is sometimes found. The final tone in a song is usually long; if it is short, the pre-final tone tends to be long. Isometric songs are not rare in Chippewa music and somewhat more common in the Menomini material, where about 30 per cent fall into that class. Most of the songs, however, are heterometric with alternations of duple and triple meter.

In this sub-area, the isorhythmic principle is more pronounced than elsewhere on the continent. This fact may account for the comparatively large number of isometric songs which are almost absent in the other sub-areas. It is this amount of isorhythmic material which distinguishes this sub-area from the others. About 30 per cent of the Chippewa songs and 45 per cent of the Menomini songs contain isorhythmic material. To be sure, only about eight per cent of the songs are completely isorhythmic, but the rest of the songs included in the above percentages exhibit some isorhythmic tendencies. Some have sections which are isorhythmic, others are isorhythmic throughout with only a few modifications, and a few are isorhythmic until the pattern is disturbed, towards the end, by the common cadential lengthening.

The rhythmic accompaniment in this sub-area is usually simple and consists of even beats throughout a song. Occasionally, the accompaniment begins a few beats before the melody, thus forming an introduction. Two variations of this technique are found: every other beat may be stressed, in contrast to the usual even dynamics; and the beating may be in triplet rhythm with beats falling on the first and third units with a rest on the second. A beat in the accompaniment is usually the same length as the average durational value in the melody, and occasionally slightly faster (e.g. the average melodic value may be 132 per minute, the drum 144 beats per minute). In a few Menomini songs a change of tempo occurs during the melody.

About 50 per cent of the songs of both tribes have progressive forms, while only 35 per cent have the incomplete repetition described above. The preponderance of the progressive forms may be due to the amount of isorhythmic material which lends a kind of structural unity to a song and makes unnecessary the unification achieved by recurring melodic material. At any rate, most of the songs with isorhythmic tendencies have progressive forms, while songs without isorhythmic material are usually not progressive. Even in the progressive forms, however, the melodic movement pattern found in the A^1 A^2 form types is present. The use of a repeated phrase at the beginning of a song is present in about one-half of the material (e.g., A A B C, A B C; or A A B C, D E).

There seems to be no organization of music into forms larger than the song with the exception of some elaborate ceremonies, such as the *mide* of the Chippewa in which the songs are in a fixed order. By far the greatest number of songs are ceremonial. Flutes (i.e., flageolets, similar to whistles or recorders) are used in this sub-area as love charms and for love songs. A number of their melodies are offered by Densmore for the Menomini. They have undulating melodic contours, the use of thirds and fourths as melodic intervals, and a range of about an octave. The forms are usually progressive or reverting.

Some of the tribes of the Southern Prairies belong together to one sub-area of the Plains-Pueblo musical area. These tribes are the Pawnee, whose general style is documented by Densmore,[4] the Osage, 137 of whose songs are published by Fletcher and LaFlesche, and the Omaha, whose music was described in an early work by Fletcher.[5] This sub-area is distinguished from the others mainly by the use of a somewhat smaller melodic range, greater variety of forms, and more variety in instrumental accompaniment. The latter is even more complex, however, in the Pueblos.

The average range of the songs in this sub-area is about an octave. Almost 50 per cent of the songs have this range. A number of songs have the range of an eleventh, about the same a perfect fifth. Ranges of two octaves are also found; the whole picture is one of great variety compared to the Chippewa-Menomini styles. The scales in this sub-area are primarily pentatonic and tetratonic. A little more than half are pentatonic. About 15 per cent of all scales contain only major and minor seconds; they are ditonic. A few ditonic, tritonic, hexatonic, and heptatonic scales are also found.

The tonic of each scale is likely to be the lowest tone, occasionally next-to-lowest (in which case it is usually a major second above the lowest). Tones next in importance to the tonic tend to be a minor third or a perfect fifth, and less often a perfect fourth, above the tonic. Occasionally important tones are found a perfect fourth below or an octave above the tonic. The most common intervals in the scales, in order of frequency, are major seconds, minor thirds, major thirds, perfect fourths, and minor seconds. A few neutral thirds, used consistently, are found (e.g. Densmore, Pawnee, No. 20).

The melodic contours are of the terrace type; this is present in 80 per cent of the material, while about 10 per cent have undulating movement. In many songs of the *hako* ceremony the terrace-type is modified: the last phrase begins as high as the first one, giving an over-all inverted arc superimposed over descent. Upward movement at the beginning of a phrase is common in this sub-area. Among the melodic intervals, major seconds predominate. Next in frequency are major and minor thirds, minor seconds, and perfect fourths, in that order. Repeated tones are common at the ends of songs, but not otherwise, in contrast to the rest of the Plains-Pueblo area.

Most of the Pawnee, Osage, and Omaha songs are dominated by two or three durational values. This restrictive tendency (in contrast with other sub-areas) is more pronounced in the songs of the Pawnee *hako,* in which only two values are sometimes found to the exclusion of others. Most of the songs are heterometric, triple and duple divisions occurring in the same song. More complex meters are rare. Triplets which contrast with regular metric divisions are common, as are

[4] Densmore, *Pawnee Music* (Bureau of American Ethnology, Bulletin 93, Washington, 1929).

[5] Alice C. Fletcher, *The Osage Tribe* (Annual Report of the Bureau of American Ethnology, 27, Washington, 1911); *A Study of Omaha Music* (Cambridge, 1893).

dotted rhythms and syncopation. The final tone in a song is usually of average length or, if short, is followed by a rest. Long tones are more likely to occur near the ends of phrases than at the beginnings. Upbeats are rare compared to the Chippewa and Menomini material.

The instrumental accompaniment is rather varied in comparison to the Chippewa and Menomini. The greatest variety is found in the songs of the *hako*. Even so, regular pulse beating is the most common. Some tremolo is found, and the alternation of stressed and unstressed drumbeats is present. Changes in the rhythm of the accompaniment during a song are found in about 15 per cent of the *hako* songs, but are rare elsewhere. These changes usually involve the replacement of regular beats by tremolo, and reversion to regular beats. A beat in the accompaniment is usually the same length as the average durational value in the melody, as are the pulsations of the voice on long tones.

The forms of Pawnee, Osage, and Omaha songs are more varied than those of the Chippewa and Menomini. The incomplete repetition type of form is comparatively rare, being present in only 30 per cent of the songs. More common here than elsewhere in the Plains-Pueblo area are reverting forms consisting of a number of short sections. These account for almost half of the songs. Most common among them is one in which an initial section is repeated, followed by a contrasting section and again by the initial one, this time transposed an octave lower: A^1 A^2 B A^3 (8). Other Pawnee forms: A^1 A^2 A^3 (8); A B C C D C; A B^1 B^2 C; A B B (common especially in the *hako*); A^1 B A^2 (8). Transposition of a section to a lower interval is common and may be carried to a rather extreme form like the following: A^1 A^1 A^1 (5) B A^2 (5) A^1 (5) A^3 (9) B. Progressive forms are found in about 10 per cent of the songs. Some isorhythmic tendencies occur, but they are less common here than in Chippewa and Menomini music. Short introductions, consisting of two or three notes on the tonic, are found in 75 per cent of the *hako* songs.

The sub-area which consists of the typical Plains tribes and some of the Northern Prairie tribes is musically the best known and documented in North America. A considerable amount of published material is available, of which the studies by Densmore on the music of Dakota[6] (240 songs), Mandan and Hidatsa[7] (110 songs), and Cheyenne and Arapaho[8] (75 songs) have been used. Manuscript studies by the writer on Arapaho music[9] (43 songs) and by Kaufman on Cheyenne music[10] (50 songs) have been analyzed. Finally, recordings of Blackfoot and Kiowa music have been studied from recordings by the writer.

The general characteristics of the Plains-Pueblo area are chrystallized in the

[6] Densmore, *Teton Sioux Music* (Bureau of American Ethnology, Bulletin **61**, Washington, 1918).

[7] Densmore, *Mandan and Hidatsa Music* (Bureau of American Ethnology, Bulletin **80**, Washington, 1923).

[8] Densmore, *Cheyenne and Arapaho Music* (Southwest Museum Papers, **10**, Los Angeles, 1936).

[9] Bruno Nettl, *Musical Culture of the Arapaho*, MA thesis, Indiana University, 1951.

[10] Howard R. Kaufman, *Cheyenne Indian Music and its Cultural Background*, MA thesis, Indiana University, 1952.

Plains sub-area; the essentials are present in greater frequency than in the other sub-areas, while the non-characteristic traits present in the sub-areas are less evident here. It is the most typical style of the Plains-Pueblo group. The range of the songs averages about a tenth. Among the Teton Dakota, Mandan, and Hidatsa it is larger than among the others. The Blackfoot songs rarely exceed an octave. The Plains are characterized by the relative frequency of tetratonic scales. Among the Teton Dakota and Cheyenne, about 30 per cent have only four tones; among the Arapaho 40 per cent. Pentatonic scales are somewhat less common than elsewhere, but they still, with the exception of the Arapaho, outnumber tetratonic ones. Tritonic scales are relatively common and are usually in some kind of triad formation: the intervals are likely to be thirds and fourths. The tonic of each scale is the lowest tone, and other important tones are a minor third, major second, or perfect fourth above it.

The intervals most common in the scales are, as elsewhere in the Plains-Pueblo area, major seconds and minor thirds. However, minor seconds are more common than in the other sub-areas. Whereas the distribution of tones in the Chippewa, Menomini, and Southern Prairie material was rather even within the scales, about half of the Plains scales have an uneven distribution of tones within the octave. A typical uneven construction, whose presence may be due to the amount of tetratonic material, is: tonic, perfect fourth, perfect fifth, major sixth, perfect octave, minor ninth (all reckoned from the tonic).

The melodic movement is almost entirely of the terrace type. The number of descents is usually less than in the Southern Prairie material; three phrases is most common as the extent of a single, long descent on the Plains and in the Menomini and Chippewa songs, while four is the rule in the Pawnee songs. The most frequent melodic intervals are major seconds and minor thirds. Perfect fourths are more common here than in the other sub-areas and are found mainly in song final position.

The rhythm of Plains songs is usually dominated by four or five durational values, all of which have approximately the same importance and frequency in a song. As a result of this, as well as of the primarily heterometric organization, which is more complex here than in the eastern sub-areas, the rhythm of Plains music appears less clear-cut and comprehensible than that of most other North American styles. Upbeats are found in about 35 per cent of the songs. Dotted rhythms are very common, while series of notes with the same value are rare. Isorhythmic organization is rarer here than in the eastern sub-areas of the Plains-Pueblo area, but it is encountered occasionally (e.g., Nettl, Arapaho, Nos. 5, 11; Densmore, Teton Dakota, Nos. 76, 138; Densmore, Mandan and Hidatsa, No. 24). Completely isorhythmic songs are very rare but isorhythmic sections are found. Isometric organization is also very rare.

The vast majority of the Plains songs have rhythmic instrumental accompaniment. It is usually slightly faster than the average note value of the melody; occasionally it is the same speed, or slightly slower. Most songs have only a simple pulse as accompaniment. Exceptions to this are the alternation of stressed and unstressed beats and triplets with rests, as described above. The latter rhythm often has a complex relationship to that of the melody; a triplet may be juxtaposed to two equal notes in the melody, and may, in addition, be slightly faster than the melody. Even beats in a syncopated relationship to the melody are found. Tremolo, especially in the use of rattles, is also present.

The most common form among the Plains Indians is the $A^1 A^2$ incomplete repetition type of form described in the introductory portion of this Section. About 75 per cent of the Teton Dakota songs, 80 per cent of the Arapaho, and 75 per cent of the Mandan and Hidatsa adhere to this type. Most of the remainder are progressive, a song usually consisting of three to five descending sections. In all of this material, repeated phrases appear more often at the beginning of a song than elsewhere. Transposition of a phrase to a lower pitch within the song occurs rather frequently in the Arapaho material: $A^1 A^1 B^1 C^1 A^2$ (2) B^2 (6) C^2 (8) B^3 (6); $A^1 B A^2$ (8) $B A^2$ (8). It should be noted that songs with meaningful texts are more likely to have the incomplete repetition form than others; songs with only meaningless syllable texts are more often progressive. This fact may be traced to the way in which the meaningful texts are usually arranged within the songs. That system is explained here, although it is common to all parts of the Plains-Pueblo area as well as some other areas; it has been studied adequately only on the Plains. The A^1 section has only meaningless syllables. The A^2 section begins with the meaningful text, which is usually not long enough to fill out the music, and ends again with meaningless syllables. Since the meaningful text of a song may be changed (the same melody with more than one text has been found by the writer among the Arapaho), and two texts of one song may not be of the same length, it is easy to fill in the remaining part of the melody with meaningless syllables, if necessary.

Some rudimentary polyphony, due to the overlapping of the end of a song with the beginning of its repetition, is found among the Arapaho. This practice is present, in all probability, also in other tribes but has not been documented. The pulsation and vocal tension which are characteristic of the Plains-Pueblo area are most developed on the Plains. The pulsations consist of small accents placed at short intervals on the longer tones. The effect is one of contrasting levels of intensity. Occasionally in the singing of women (where vocal tension is less), this contrast carries over into pitch. A long tone may have the effect of a slow trill which begins with a downward movement. Strong glissandos are used, especially at the end of a phrase or song. The vocal tension gives rise to short, accented ornamental tones which occur before the longer tones of the melody and sometimes resemble shrieks.

The style of the Pueblos is the most complex in North America (with the probable exception of the Mexican high cultures). It has been described as a whole by Herzog,[11] who includes 38 transcriptions in his study. Some early works on the music of individual Pueblos were made by Gilman,[12] and a later one is by

---

[11] George Herzog, "A Comparison of Pueblo and Pima Musical Styles," *JAF*, 49 (1938), 283-417.

[12] Benjamin Ives Gilman, "Hopi Songs," *Journal of American Ethnology and Archeology*, 5 (1908), 1-160; "Zuni Melodies," *Journal of American Ethnology and Archeology*, 1 (1891), 63-91.

Densmore,[13] who includes 102 transcriptions. Curtis-Burlin[14] includes 22 Pueblo songs in her collection. Roberts[15] has published transcriptions and analyses of Picurís songs.

Herzog distinguishes, in degree of complexity, between the Eastern (Tanoan) and the Western (Hopi, Zuni, and Keresan) Pueblos; the greatest complexity is found in the West, while the Eastern Pueblos have a style intermediate between those of the Western ones and the Plains. The range of Pueblo songs averages about a tenth. It is rarely less than an octave and not often over a twelfth. The scales tend to have more tones than those of the Plains sub-area. Pentatonic scales, to be sure, are in the majority; next in frequency are hexatonic scales, with heptatonic ones more common, and tetratonic ones less, than in the other sub-areas. Important tones in the scales tend to be separated by intervals of a perfect fourth or a perfect fifth. The tonic is usually the lowest tone and sometimes (more frequently than on the Plains) the next-to-lowest. The main intervals in the scales are major and minor seconds and minor thirds; especially in the Western Pueblos do minor seconds play an important role in the scales, although they are melodically less important.

The predominant direction of the melody is downward. A large number of songs, especially in the Eastern Pueblos, exhibit the terrace type of melodic movement. In the Eastern Pueblos the melody oscillates between tones wider apart, while in the West the direction of the movement changes frequently, the melody moving in smaller intervals. Characteristic of the West is the division of a song into two main parts each of which has its own scale and tonal organization. The second part often starts higher than the first. Within each part, however, the terrace and descending types of melodic movement predominate. In spite of this primacy of downward movement, ascending movement is more common in the Pueblos than elsewhere in the Plains-Pueblo area. The most common melodic intervals are, as elsewhere, minor thirds and major seconds, with perfect fourths and fifths prominent.

The rhythm of Pueblo songs is complex; each song is dominated by several different values (usually five or six) which occur in alternating successions; the same note value is only rarely repeated. Isometric organization is exceedingly rare; Herzog stresses the importance of "final lengthening;" rhythmic units tend to be longer in phrase final or song final position than at initial points. Triplets and dotted rhythms are common, isorhythmic organization absent.

Herzog distinguishes three types of rhythmic accompaniment, which phase of music is again the most complex in the Pueblos (with the possible exception of the Northwest Coast). The first, more common in the East, consists of a simple continuity of beats which is broken by rests at points of rest in the melody. The second type is more expressive of the rhythmic structure of the melody, varying the basic pulse in accordance with the rhythmic changes in the melody. In the third type the

[13] Densmore, *Music of Santo Domingo Pueblo* (Southwest Museum Papers, **12**, Los Angeles, 1938).

[14] Natalie Curtis-Burlin, *The Indians' Book* (New York and London, 1907).

[15] Helen H. Roberts, "Analysis of Picurís Songs" (Annual Report of the Bureau of American Ethnology, **43**, Washington, 1928), 399-447.

single beats in the melody and the accompaniment do not coincide except at the beginnings of rhythmic design units. Tremolo is used sometimes as the introduction of a song, before the melody begins.

The forms of the Pueblo songs are great in number and complexity. Most common are various types related to the incomplete and modified repetition forms of the area in general; iterative and reverting elements appear within the larger units. Examples: A^1 /: A^2 B B :/ (Herzog, No. 5); A A B C D B C D (Herzog, No. 9); A^1 /: A^2 B^1 B^2 C D :/ (Herzog, No. 6). The most complex forms appear in the Western Pueblos. Some songs (especially katchina songs) consist of two distinct parts which are designated as "verse" and "chorus" by native singers when they speak English: Verse—A^1 B^1 A^2 B^2; Chorus—C D E F G H^1 H^2 (Herzog, No. 23). The use of introductory and connecting phrases which commonly play on only one tone (usually the tonic) are common; although they are found on the Plains, their development in the Pueblos is much more complex. They are used primarily between the major sections of the incomplete repetition form type. The largest organization of music, above the song level, is the song series which consists of all the material for a given ceremony and whose order is fixed.

The vocal technique of the Pueblos is similar to that of the Plains, with one important exception: singing in a low voice with a growling quality is considered desirable in the Pueblo katchina songs in contrast to the Plains, where high voices are generally considered best.

The Pima and Papago are, from the standpoint of musical style, marginal to the Plains-Pueblo area. Their style may be described as a combination of Plains-Pueblo elements with some of the California-Yuman area, the nature of which is indicated in the summary below.

The traits which serve to unify the musical styles of the Plains-Pueblo area are discussed in the introductory portion of this Section. It remains to summarize the traits by which the several sub-areas are distinguished. The most typical of the sub-areas is that of the Plains. It is characterized by the terrace type of melodic movement, extreme vocal tension and pulsation in the vocal technique, complex rhythmic organization dominated by several durational values, and a considerable proportion of tetratonic scales.

The Chippewa and Menomini styles are differentiated from the Plains style by the use of larger ranges and a considerable amount of isorhythmic material. The Southern Prairie tribes show some relationship to the music of the Southeastern United States. The songs are characterized by a greater variety of forms, including some consisting of several short sections which are interwoven in reverting and iterative relationships, as well as the use of relatively few durational values and some isometric tendencies.

The most complex sub-area is that of the Pueblos. It is characterized by a greater variety of forms most of which are relatively long, more complex tonal organization, including the use of many hexatonic scales, and the use of contours other than the terrace type. The complexity is greatest in the Western Pueblos, while the Eastern ones show closer relationships to Plains music.

The Pima and Papago style combines some traits of the Plains-Pueblo area with those of the California-Yuman area. The Plains-Pueblo traits are large range, descending melodic movement, complex rhythmic organization, and some form types. With the California-Yuman area they share a relaxed vocal technique, general structural simplicity, and an elaborate system of ideas on music. It also has the Yuman organization of songs in long cycles.

The music of some Plateau tribes (Kutenai, Flathead, and Nez Perce) may be a part of this musical area; if this is true, they probably would be most closely allied with the Plains sub-area. But the style of the Plateau material is not well enough known to enable the writer to place these tribes definitely within a musical area.

7. THE EASTERN AREA

The area including the Southeastern United States and the East Coast of the continent as far north as Labrador belongs, in all probability, to one musical area. The styles of the Southeast are relatively well documented, but material from the Middle Atlantic and New England areas, as well as Eastern Canada, is rather scarce. This is true more of the Algonquian tribes than the Iroquois. In the Southeast, the Creek and Yuchi[16] (151 songs), the Choctaw[17] (65 songs), and the Tutelo[18] (28 songs) are represented by monographs. The music of the Shawnee, which is to some extent marginal to this area, has been studied by the writer.[19] Iroquois songs have been transcribed by Cringan[20] (48 songs) in an early study and described more recently by Kurath.[21] The only substantial group of transcriptions from the Northern Algonquian tribes is that of Speck (Sapir)[22] on Penobscot music. Curtis-Burlin has published 12 Abnaki songs.

Simplicity of musical style is greatest in the northern part of the Eastern area, while the South is relatively complex. The main characteristics are undulating melodic movement, relatively short songs (some as short as ten seconds), the use of forms which consist of several short sections with iterative and reverting relationships, relative simplicity and asymmetry in the rhythmic organization, and, perhaps the most distinctive feature, antiphonal and responsorial technique and some rudimentary polyphony including, possibly, imitation and canon. Although there is considerable difference between the tribal styles, the entire area is relatively homogeneous and need not be divided into sub-areas.

The ranges of the Eastern area are relatively smaller than those of the Plains-Pueblo area, and could be considered average for the continent as a whole. Among the Penobscot and Iroquois an octave is normal. In the Southeast the average is about a sixth. The number of tones in the scales varies considerably from tribe to

[16] Frank G. Speck, *Ceremonial Songs of the Creek and Yuchi Indians* (Philadelphia, 1911).

[17] Densmore, *Choctaw Music* (Bureau of American Ethnology, Bulletin **136**, Anthropological Papers, 28, Washington, 1943), 101-108.

[18] Speck, *The Tutelo Spirit Adoption Ceremony* (Harrisburg, 1942).

[19] Bruno Nettl, "The Shawnee Musical Style: Historical Perspective in Primitive Music," *Southwestern Journal of Anthropology*, 9 (1953), 277-285.

[20] Alexander T. Cringan, "Music of the Pagan Iroquois," *Archaeological Report* (Toronto, 1899).

[21] The writer wishes to express his gratitude to Gertrude P. Kurath for permission to examine her large collection of Iroquois transcriptions.

[22] Speck, *Penobscot Man* (Philadelphia, 1940).

tribe. The Penobscot scales are predominantly hexatonic and heptatonic. The Iroquois scales are mainly pentatonic, with major seconds and minor thirds the most important intervals. The Tutelo scales are also predominantly pentatonic with tetratonic scales also prominent. Here, again, major seconds, minor thirds, and perfect fourths are common. The scales of the Choctaw are mainly pentatonic and tetratonic. Of the Yuchi and Creek scales, about 80 percent are pentatonic and tetratonic, but tritonic and ditonic scales, as well as some with only one tone (e.g., Speck, Creek and Yuchi, Nos. 1 and 4) are also found. It should be noted that in Speck's publication a number of series of short songs, each designated by a letter, are presented. The intervals in Creek and Yuchi scales also vary; major seconds are most frequent and minor seconds comparatively common.

The tonic in all styles is the lowest tone in about 35 per cent, next-to-lowest in 30 per cent, and higher in the remainder of the songs. In a few the tonic is the highest tone. Other important tones are usually above the tonic at distances of perfect fourths, fifths, and octaves.

The melodic movement in the Eastern area is primarily undulating; there is somewhat more descent than ascent. A specialized kind of movement found in a few songs is the Rise, common in the California-Yuman area. It is found in the Penobscot and Choctaw material to a considerable extent and more rarely in that of the other Eastern tribes. The melodic intervals are most frequently major seconds and minor thirds. Others, in order of their frequency, are perfect fourths, major thirds, minor seconds, and perfect fifths. Octave jumps are found.

The rhythmic organization of the Eastern area is more symmetrical and simpler than that of the Plains-Pueblo area, and is comparable, in complexity, with that of the California-Yuman area. The songs are usually dominated by two or three durational values. An exception to this are the Penobscot songs where four to six note values are distributed about evenly within each song. Triplets are moderately common; dotted rhythms with the longer note first are found. The final tones of songs are usually short or average followed by a rest. Sometimes they are long, and not followed by a rest. Pre-final tones tend to be long if the final ones are short. Isometric organization is common; it is found in about one-half of the songs. Again, the Penobscot are an exception; their songs are predominantly heterometric. Meter is more likely to be duple than triple. Consistent use of complex meters, such as five-eighths or seven-eighths, is found occasionally.

Some use of the isorhythmic principle is present, although entirely isorhythmic songs are rare. Use of isorhythmic patterns which are not broken until the final phrases of a song is more common in the southern part of the area. The introduction of minor variations into an otherwise isorhythmic section is common.

Most of the transcribed songs are notated without rhythmic accompaniment. Although this is not indicative of actual performance practices, it is probable that rhythmic accompaniment is less universal here than in the Plains-Pueblo area. Where rhythmic accompaniment is found, it is usually a simple pulse which coincides with the basic pulse of the melody. The accompaniment may rest when the voice rests. The use of tremolo, especially in the playing of rattles, is also found. Among the Iroquois conscious contrast between ordinary beating and tremolo is found. For example, in the songs of the Eagle Dance, whose form is almost always A A B A B, the A sections are accompanied by tremolo, the B sections by a steady pulse. The over-all rhythmic picture in the Eastern area is, then, that of relatively clear-cut organization which is much easier to perceive for the Western European listener than is that of the Plains-Pueblo area.

The forms of the Eastern area, on the other hand, are generally more varied and sometimes more complex than those of the Plains-Pueblo area. Although they are often short (the average is shorter than that of the latter), they usually consist of a number of different parts which are interwoven in various ways. The over-all formal organization in Eastern music is usually a song series consisting of a few (six, eight, or less) songs with a fixed order. In some cases a series is sung without interruption.

The simplest forms in the Eastern area are those which consist of one short motif repeated several times. These are found among the Creek (e.g., Speck, Nos. 4 and 5). It is in these songs that antiphonal and responsorial techniques are prominent; the single phrase is sung alternately by a leader and a group, or by two individuals, with minor variations.

The typical forms of the Eastern area are more complex and are illustrated by the following examples: A^1 A^1 B^1 A^1 C^1 A^1 B^2 C^2 C^3 A^2 (Densmore, Choctaw, No. 7); A B A B C B D B (Choctaw, No. 58); A B C A C, C D, A B C A C (Choctaw, No. 21); A B A C A C A A A (Speck, Tutelo, No. 1); A B C D C (Tutelo, No. 24); A B A B C C A B C (Cringan, Iroquois, No. 16); A B C D C A (Iroquois, No. 28); A A B^1 A A A B^2 (Speck, Penobscot, p. 282); A^1 B A^1 C D A^2 B A^1 (Penobscot, p. 279). The incomplete repetition type of form characteristic of the Plains-Pueblo area is found in about 15 per cent of the Eastern area songs. Within each main section of this form, however, are found iterative and reverting elements, in contrast to the usually progressive forms of the same sections on the Plains. The most common manifestation of this type is among the Iroquois: A A B A B. Some purely progressive forms are found (e.g., Densmore, Choctaw, Nos. 18 and 23) and a few songs have the paired-phrase patterns of the Great Basin musical area, in which each phrase is repeated. The phrases in the songs here are likely to be approximately the same length within each song, and they are usually shorter than those of the other musical areas.

Antiphonal and responsorial singing have been introduced above. Although a few songs consist of this kind of alternate singing of short phrases only, these techniques are mainly associated with call-like or yell-like phrases (with fixed pitches) at the beginnings, and, more often, at the ends of songs. This is found with considerable frequency in all the tribes of the Eastern area whose music has been examined.

Some rudimentary polyphony is based on antiphonal and responsorial techniques. When the answering phrase is begun before the initial one has been concluded, a type of round has come into existence. This kind of canon singing, although it seems to have originated accidentally, has been stylized and fixed to a degree. The writer has neither heard recordings nor seen transcriptions of it, but it has been described by some early writers and travelers. Drone type of polyphony, in which a single long pitch is juxtaposed to the melody, is also mentioned. None of the descriptions give any information about the resulting harmonic intervals;

it may be assumed that the imitation was not of the close variety since it originated with the overlapping of only a tone or two at the end of a phrase.

The vocal technique of the Eastern area is intermediate between that of the Plains-Pueblo area and that of Western European music. Some use of pulsation on the longer tones is found, but the singing is more relaxed than on the Plains. Of all the Eastern tribes studied, the Iroquois approach most closely the vocal technique of the Plains-Pueblo area.

8. SUMMARY AND CONCLUSIONS

Six musical areas have been identified and described, of unequal size, but justified by the fact that each of them is characterized by several traits which are relatively specialized. A list of the most important traits of each area is given here.

Eskimo-Northwest Coast area: 1. average range a major sixth; 2. undulating and pendulum types of melodic movement; 3. importance of minor seconds, major thirds, and perfect fourths as melodic intervals in contrast to other areas; 4. recitative-like singing with uncertain pitches and monotonic sections; 5. rhythmic complexity; 6. rhythmic design in the instrumental accompaniment; 7. complex relationships between melodic and percussive rhythms; 8. looseness, flexibility of form, and use of throughcomposed forms; 9. responsorial technique; 10. drone type of polyphony.

Great Basin area: 1. small melodic range; 2. undulating melodic movement; 3. some recitative used to narrate myths; 4. tonic is final tone of most phrases; 5. many songs without any percussive accompaniment; 6. paired-phrase patterns in form; 7. relaxed, non-pulsating vocal technique.

California-Yuman area: 1. average range an octave; 2. undulating or gradually descending melodic contour; 3. isometric organization common; 4. use of the Rise in the majority of songs; 5. frequency of isorhythmic material; 6. forms intermediate between strophic and throughcomposed; 7. long song series the largest unit of organization; 8. relatively relaxed and non-pulsating vocal technique.

Athabascan area: 1. great variety in range: from perfect fifth to two octaves; 2. arc-shaped melodic contour; 3. large melodic intervals: fifths, sixths, octaves; 4. use of only two durational values in each song; 5. considerable amount of isometric material; 6. use of falsetto.

Plains-Pueblo area: 1. large range (average a tenth); 2. terrace type of melodic contour; 3. complex rhythmic organization; 4. considerable proportion of tetratonic scales; 5. incomplete repetition type of form; 6. much vocal tension and heavy pulsation.

Eastern area: 1. average range about an octave; 2. undulating and gradually descending melodic movement; 3. more hexatonic and heptatonic scales than elsewhere in North America; 4. use of two or three main durational values; 5. some isometric and isorhythmic construction; 6. forms consisting of several short sections in iterative, and reverting relationships; 7. short songs; 8. antiphonal and responsorial techniques; 9. yells before and after a song; 10. some polyphony of the imitative and drone types; 11. moderate amount of vocal tension and pulsations.

As has been stated in Section 1, relative complexity of style has not been taken into consideration in identifying the musical areas. In several of them there are both simple and complex styles. It should be noted that the most complex styles, those of the Pueblos, the Northwest Coast, and the Gulf of Mexico, are located in the three largest musical areas.

The most typical style within an area is not always found in its geographic center, although this is occasionally the case. In some of them it is difficult to find the typical style, i.e., that style in which the area's most essential features are found with the greatest intensity. In the case of the Plains-Pueblo area the Plains style seems to be the most typical, and it is located in the central portion of the musical area. In this area it is relatively easy to find a "most typical" style because of the number of sub-areas which is sufficiently great to afford a contrast among them, while in some of the other areas this is more difficult because of the lack of documentation. It is unusual, nevertheless, for the typical styles in the areas to appear at the geographic limits of the areas. On the contrary, the areas do not have distinct borders, and the tribes at the limits of some of the areas sometimes share important musical traits with both adjoining areas. This is similar in nature to the culture areas as discussed by Wissler and treated further below.

Neither the most complex nor the simplest styles of a musical area can be said to follow any set pattern in their geographic location within their area. It might be expected that the most complex manifestation of a style would be found at the center of its distribution, while the simplest would be found at the limits. This is only sometimes the case. In the Eskimo-Northwest Coast area the simplest style, that of the Eskimo, is at one geographic extreme, while the most complex, that of the Northwest Coast tribes, is more centrally located. A similar situation is found in the Great Basin area: the simplest style, that of the Modoc and Klamath, is on the margin of the area. In the case of the Plains-Pueblo area, however, the opposite is found. Perhaps the simplest style here is that of the Plains tribes, centrally located, while the most complex, that of the Pueblos, is on the fringe. These examples demonstrate the difficulty of making generalizations about the relative locations of the typical, complex, and simple styles within a musical area.

The musical areas are based, as has been pointed out, on the features of the musical styles alone. The distributions of musical instruments and of traits concerning the cultural background of the music have not been considered. The areas based on the latter considerations would be different from those found here and would perhaps coincide with the culture areas to a greater degree than do the musical areas. A few notable exceptions to these generalizations concern the coincidence of some features of the cultural background of music with some stylistic sub-areas. For example, the use of fairly well developed musical terminology, the practice of rehearsing, and the punishment of musical errors coincide with the Northwest Coast sub-area. However, it should be emphasized that elaborate systems of musical terminology and ideas about music do not always coincide with complex styles. Such fairly elaborate systems are found in California, among the Yuman tribes and among the Pima, all of which have about an average degree of complexity. As far as is known, some centers of musical complexity, such as the Pueblos and the Southeastern United States, do not have any elaborate systems of musical thought.

The musical areas correspond in some ways, and fail to correspond in others, with the culture areas, both in their nature, as has been demonstrated, and in their geographic boundaries. While it is possible to find musical centers of the greatest development and complexity within each of the musical areas, these do not always coincide with the most typical—perhaps the most specialized—musical style within an area. These centers are enumerated above; they are not always in the geographic centers of the musical areas. A good example of the musical analogue to Wissler's "intermediate cultures" between two culture centers are the styles called marginal in this study. Although only a few tribes can be designated as such, it is probable that the knowledge of more musical styles on the continent would enable a whole series of them to be identified. Of those in this study, the Pima-Papago style is intermediate between the California-Yuman and the Plains-Pueblo areas; the Northern Ute style is intermediate between the Great Basin and the Plains-Pueblo styles; and the Shawnee style is intermediate between the Eastern and Plains-Pueblo styles. The styles of some Plateau tribes (Nez Perce, Flathead, Kutenai) may be intermediate between the Eskimo-Northwest Coast and the Plains-Pueblo styles.

The arrangement of the musical areas coincides in a general way with those of the culture areas of Wissler [23] and Kroeber, [24] but not at specific geographic points. It is difficult to make boundaries for the musical areas, just as it is hard to delimit the culture areas exactly, especially since the musical styles of all individual tribes are not known in detail. The musical areas are compared, in the following paragraphs, with Wissler's culture areas and then with those of Kroeber. Wissler's number of culture areas (nine) indicates smaller divisions than are found for the musical areas. None of his areas coincide exactly with any of the musical areas, but some of them form musical sub-areas. His subdivision of the Woodlands culture area into three parts (Iroquois, Eastern, and Central) also reflects musical differences. The Central Woodlands belong primarily to the Plains-Pueblo area, while the Iroquois and the Eastern Woodlands are part of the Eastern area.

A somewhat closer relationship is found between the musical areas and Kroeber's culture areas, whose identification is more recent than Wissler's. Kroeber has five main areas (in addition to Middle America); these are larger and correspond in size somewhat more closely to the musical areas than do Wissler's culture areas. The Arctic Coast is one of Kroeber's primary areas; it corresponds to the Eskimo sub-area of the Eskimo-Northwest Coast musical area. Kroeber's Northwest Coast culture area makes up the rest of this musical area with the exception of a few Salish tribes who are in his Intermediate-Intermountain area.

The Intermediate-Intermountain culture area is not, in contrast to Kroeber's others, believed to be a substantial unit of historical development or of a prevailing characteristic current of culture. Its heterogeneous cultural nature is also reflected in its musical characteristics. It contains parts of four musical areas: 1. the northern part of the California-Yuman, 2. a small eastern part of the Eskimo-Northwest Coast, 3. a very small part of the Plains-Pueblo (in the Plateau region),

---

[23] Clark Wissler, *The American Indian* (New York, 1922) pp. 218-242.

[24] A. L. Kroeber, *Cultural and Natural Areas in Native North America* (Berkeley and Los Angeles, 1947) pp. 20-108.

and 4. the entire Great Basin. Kroeber's division of this primary area into three secondary areas fits the musical picture more closely. His Great Basin area coincides almost exactly with the Great Basin musical area; the Californian section contains only parts, however, of the California-Yuman musical area. The Columbia-Frazer area contains some Plains-Pueblo as well as some Salish styles.

Kroeber's Southwest area is musically also heterogeneous. It contains parts of the Plains-Pueblo area, the Navaho and Apache of the Athabascan area, and the southern and eastern parts of the California-Yuman area. His main subdivisions here, the Yuman tribes on the one hand and the Pueblos and Athabascans on the other, coincide with the musical picture. Indeed, the Athabascan and Pueblo styles are related if contrasted with the California-Yuman style.

The remainder of the continent is united by Kroeber in one large culture area, containing the McKenzie, Plains, Woodlands, and Southeastern areas of Wissler. The musical areas represented here are the northern part of the Plains-Pueblo, and the entire Eastern areas. Kroeber's main subdivisions of this large area are the Northern Athabascans and the Algonquian tribes north of the Great Lakes juxtaposed to the remainder. This division may have musical parallels, but it is as yet too little known in its northern section.

While the musical areas do not coincide specifically with the culture areas of Wissler and Kroeber, it has been shown that the cultural divisions, both primary and secondary, are relevant to the musical areas and sub-areas. The general distribution over the continent is similar: in both general culture and music, the East is more homogeneous than the West. The eastern areas are larger and less than the ones in the western portion of the continent.

Since the discussion of the geographic size of the musical areas without consideration of population density may be misleading, the writer has computed approximate population figures for each of the musical areas based on the tribal estimates of Kroeber.[25] They apply, of course, to conditions at contact times and are highly tentative, especially since there is a margin of error in the original estimate as well as in the designation of tribes within musical areas. Nevertheless, the entire North American population (except for Mexico) has been included in the total; the tribes whose styles are not known have been assigned to the areas to which they are most likely, in the opinion of the writer, to belong. The population for each area is given in the following list: Eskimo-Northwest Coast, 267,000; Great Basin, 30,000; California-Yuman, 128,000; Athabascan, 95,000; Plains-Pueblo, 220,000; Eastern, 275,000; Total, 1,015,000. Attention is called to the relatively low number of participants in North American Indian music as a whole. Three of the musical areas take up 75 per cent of the population. These are the areas with the most complex musical styles (Pueblo, Northwest Coast, and Southeastern United States). It should be noted, furthermore, that the Plains-Pueblo area, whose style has been considered as the most typical of North America, and whose area is largest on the map, is only third in order of population size. Of further interest is the fact that of the three areas with the smallest population, the largest, California-Yuman, has the most complex style while the smallest, Great Basin, has the sim-

[25] Kroeber, 1947, p. 142.

plest. There is positive correlation, all along the line, between population size and musical complexity of the musical areas.

It is relevant also to compare the population density of the musical areas with their relative complexity. The greatest density is found in the Pueblos. Relatively great density is found also in California, on the Northwest Coast, and in the Southeastern United States, most of which are centers of complexity (except California). The centers of population, then, are also centers of musical development. There seems to be no correlation, however, between the population size of a given tribe and its musical complexity. The three points of most complex musical development coincide approximately with the three centers of greatest cultural intensity, according to Kroeber.

The musical picture does not coincide, however, with that of the areas occupied by speakers of specific language families. Most of the musical areas contain representatives of a number of language families, and many language families (at least the larger ones) have representatives in more than one musical area. A few notable exceptions to this have been found. The Eskimo sub-area is occupied entirely by the Eskimo-Aleut language family. The Great Basin musical area contains primarily (but not exclusively) tribes speaking Shoshonean languages of the Uto-Aztecan family. The only musical area which coincides almost entirely with one language family is the Athabascan. Even here the coincidence is not complete, since some Athabascan-speaking tribes on the Northwest Coast are part of the Eskimo-Northwest Coast area. It should be noted, however, that the Athabascan musical area coincides generally with the language family in spite of the fact that it is not contiguous; it is found in two large divisions, one in Western Canada and one in the Southwestern United States, as is the language family. The linguistic relationship of these two groups of tribes indicates that at one time they were in contact with each other and must have shared many culture traits; they do not have similar cultures today, however. Musical style is one of the few. This would lead to the conclusion that musical style features survive, in some cases, longer than do most other culture traits. It is unfortunate that more is not known of the style of the Northern Athabascans; however, since they are largely unknown, such conclusions must be reserved until greater knowledge has been acquired.

The six linguistic structural types identified by the Voegelins[26] also do not coincide with the musical areas, with the exception of Type I, which includes only the Eskimo sub-area. On the other hand, even a musical sub-area of such homogeneity as the Plains includes members of the Athabascan (Kiowa Apache), Algonquian (Blackfoot, Cheyenne, Arapaho), Siouan (Crow, Teton Dakota, Mandan, Hidatsa), Kiowa, and Uto-Aztecan (Comanche) language families.

The comparison of the musical areas with both culture and language areas has yielded a mixture of results. Both similarities and differences between the various systems have been found. The picture of the musical distributions in relation to the culture areas is one of general similarity but specific difference. The similarities are greater between the culture and musical areas than between the language and

[26] Carl F. Voegelin and Erminie W. Voegelin, *Map of North American Indian Languages* (Publications of the American Ethnological Society, 20).

musical areas. In the latter comparison, however, some similarities also have been found; these contradict (in the case of the Athabascans, for example), supplement, and perhaps help to explain some of the differences between musical and culture areas.

The six musical areas identified in this study are not isolated units; undoubtedly there has been interchange of stylistic traits among them. These traits probably reached America from primarily two directions: the north and northwest, ultimately Asia, and from the south, the high cultures of Mexico and Middle America. What features came from which of these places can at present not be stated with any hope of accuracy. It seems probable that antiphonal and responsorial techniques as well as polyphony came from Mexico, or that at least the stimulus for them came from the evidently complex music of the Aztecs and Mayas. It is probable that the descending melodic movement, the rhythmic complexity, and the strictly strophic forms came from the north, but this is very tentative. Three centers of musically great complexity and highest development are found: the Northwest Coast, the Pueblos, and the Southeastern United States. It is likely that the Southeastern United States is the climax of the Mexican-influenced developments, that the Pueblos represent the culmination of the northern influences, and that the Northwest Coast shared in both to a degree which caused it to develop great complexity along some lines of both major currents. These two main influences with their culminations in three centers of complexity may be the main trends of the history of North American Indian music. They are offered here as a speculative hypothesis on the genesis of American Indian music, but they are not established and should not be taken as definitive.

All of the statements about areas and distributions made in this study are subject to revision. Many of them are based on hardly adequate source material and are speculative. There is still a great need for monographs on many individual tribes and groups of tribes. However, the material presented here has been sufficient to outline the general stylistic boundaries and to indicate some of the currents which prevailed in the development of North American Indian music.

APPENDIX OF MUSICAL EXAMPLES

SPECIAL SYMBOLS USED IN THE EXAMPLES

+   above a note: about a quarter-tone higher than noted.

-      above a note: about a quarter-tone lower than noted.

(♩)   pitch uncertain.

♩, ♩   pitch quite indefinite, but in the neighborhood of the end of the stem.

♪   grace note, without rhythmic significance.

♩ ♩ ♩   dynamically weak tones.

♩ ♩   pulsations on longer tones, without an actual break in the sound.

♩♩ ♩♩   strong tie, unites all notes with the same syllable glide, glissando.

⌒   above a note: slightly longer than noted.

⌣   above a note: slightly shorter than noted.

    full bar-line: major rhythmic division or structural division.

    half bar-line: minor rhythmic division.

1. Padleirmiut Eskimo:

Z. Estreicher, "Die Musik der Eskimos," *Anthropos,* 45 (1950), song No. 6.

2. Eskimo Drum Rhythms:

Thuren and Thalbitzer, *On The Eskimo Music* (Copenhagen, 1911), p. 13.

3. Thompson River:

Abraham and Hornbostel, "Phonographierte Indianermelodien aus Britisch Columbia," *Boas Anniversary Volume* (New York, 1906), song No. 34.

4. Thompson River:

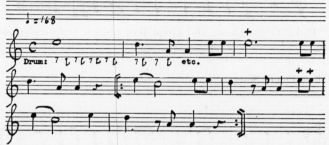

Abraham and Hornbostel, "Phonographierte Indianermelodien aus Britisch Columbia," *Boas Anniversary Volume* (New York, 1906), song No. 34.

5. Tsimshian:

Garfield, Wingert, and Barbeau, *The Tsimshian: Their Arts and Music* (New York, n.d.), song No. 5.

6. Paiute:

Herzog, "Plains Ghost Dance and Great Basin Music," *American Anthropologist,* **37** (1935), 419.

7. Arapaho Ghost Dance Song:

Recorded by James Mooney, deposited at Indiana University; transcribed by the author.

8. Shawnee Song from a Myth:

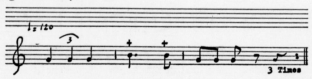

Recorded by C.F. and E.W. Voegelin, deposited at Indiana University; transcribed by the author.

9. Modoc:

Recorded by Leslie Spier, deposited at Indiana University; transcribed by J. C. Hall.

10. Modoc:

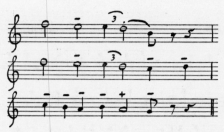

Recorded by Leslie Spier, deposited at Indiana University; transcribed by J. C. Hall.

11. Mohave:

Densmore, *Yuman and Yaqui Music* (Washington, 1932), p. 82.

12. Yuma:

Densmore, *Yuman and Yaqui Music* (Washington, 1932), p. 99.

13. Navaho:

Herzog, "Speech-Melody and Primitive Music," *Musical Quarterly,* **20** (1934), 460.

14. Navaho:

Recorded by Laura Boulton, published on Victor record album, *Indian Music of the Southwest;* transcribed by the author.

15. Arapaho Peyote Song:

Recorded by Z. Salzmann, deposited at Indiana University; transcribed by the author.

16. Arapaho Peyote Song:

Recorded and transcribed by the author; deposited at Indiana University.

17. Menominee:

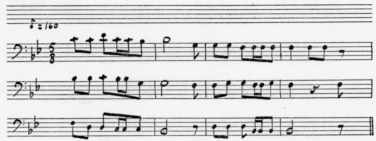

Densmore, *Menominee Music* (Washington, 1932), p. 73.

18. Pawnee:

Alice Fletcher, *The Hako* (Washington, 1904), p. 97.

19. Arapaho (excerpt showing antiphonal technique):

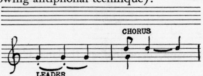

Recorded by Z. Salzmann, deposited at Indiana University; transcribed by the author.

20. Arapaho:

Recorded and transcribed by the author; deposited at Indiana University.

21. Arapaho:

    Recorded by Z. Salzmann, deposited at Indiana University; transcribed by the author.

22. Blackfoot:

    Recorded and transcribed by the author; deposited at Indiana University.

23. Santo Domingo Pueblo:

    Densmore, *Music of Santo Domingo Pueblo* (Los Angeles, 1938), p. 159.

24. Papago Flute Melody:

Densmore, *Papago Music* (Washington, 1929), p. 217.

25. Shawnee:

Recorded by C.F. and E.W. Voegelin, deposited at Indiana University; transcribed by the author.

26. Shawnee:

Recorded by C.F. and E.W. Voegelin, deposited at Indiana University; transcribed by the author.

27. Choctaw:

Densmore, *Choctaw Music* (Washington, 1943), p. 159.

28. Iroquois:

Gertrude Kurath, in W.N. Fenton, ed., *Symposium on Local Diversity in Iroquois Culture* (Washington, 1951), p. 124.